Lemony Snicket
(Daniel Handler)

WHO
WROTE
THAT?

WHO
WROTE
THAT?

Lemony Snicket
(Daniel Handler)

Dennis Abrams

Foreword by
Kyle Zimmer

CHELSEA HOUSE
PUBLISHERS
An imprint of Infobase Publishing

Lemony Snicket (Daniel Handler)

J-B
SNICKET
395-5211

Library of Congress Cataloging-in-Publication Data
Abrams, Dennis, 1960-
 Lemony Snicket (Daniel Handler) / Dennis Abrams.
 p. cm. — (Who wrote that?)
 Includes bibliographical references and index.
 ISBN 978-1-60413-726-2
 1. Handler, Daniel—Juvenile literature. 2. Snicket, Lemony. Series of unfortunate events—Juvenile literature. 3. Authors, American—20th century——Biography—Juvenile literature. I. Title. II. Series.
 PS3558.A4636Z55 2010
 813'.54—dc22
 [B]   2010006599

Text design by Keith Trego
Cover design by Alicia Post
Composition by EJB Publishing Services
Cover printed by Bang Printing, Brainerd, MN
Book printed and bound by Bang Printing, Brainerd, MN
Date printed: November 2010
Printed in the United States of America

10 9 8 7 6 5 4 3 2 1

This book is printed on acid-free paper.

Table of Contents

FOREWORD BY
KYLE ZIMMER
PRESIDENT, FIRST BOOK

HUMANITY IS POWERED by stories. From our earliest days as thinking beings, we employed every available tool to tell each other stories. We danced, drew pictures on the walls of our caves, spoke, and sang. All of this extraordinary effort was designed to entertain, recount the news of the day, explain natural occurrences—and then gradually to build religious and cultural traditions and establish the common bonds and continuity that eventually formed civilizations. Stories are the most powerful force in the universe; they are the primary element that has distinguished our evolutionary path.

Our love of the story has not diminished with time. Enormous segments of societies are devoted to the art of storytelling. Book sales in the United States alone topped $24 billion in 2006; movie studios spend fortunes to create and promote stories; and the news industry is more pervasive in its presence than ever before.

There is no mystery to our fascination. Great stories are magic. They can introduce us to new cultures, or remind us of the nobility and failures of our own, inspire us to greatness or scare us to death; but above all, stories provide human insight on a level that is unavailable through any other source. In fact, stories connect each of us to the rest of humanity not just in our own time, but also throughout history.

This special magic of books is the greatest treasure that we can hand down from generation to generation. In fact, that spark in a child that comes from books became the motivation for the creation of my organization, First Book, a national literacy program with a simple mission: to provide new books to the most disadvantaged children. At present, First Book has been at work in hundreds of communities for over a decade. Every year children in need receive millions of books through our organization and millions more are provided through dedicated literacy institutions across the United States and around the world. In addition, groups of people dedicate themselves tirelessly to working with children to share reading and stories in every imaginable setting from schools to the streets. Of course, this Herculean effort serves many important goals. Literacy translates to productivity and employability in life and many other valid and even essential elements. But at the heart of this movement are people who love stories, love to read, and want desperately to ensure that no one misses the wonderful possibilities that reading provides.

When thinking about the importance of books, there is an overwhelming urge to cite the literary devotion of great minds. Some have written of the magnitude of the importance of literature. Amy Lowell, an American poet, captured the concept when she said, "Books are more than books. They are the life, the very heart and core of ages past, the reason why men lived and worked and died, the essence and quintessence of their lives." Others have spoken of their personal obsession with books, as in Thomas Jefferson's simple statement: "I live for books." But more compelling, perhaps, is the almost instinctive excitement in children for books and stories.

Throughout my years at First Book, I have heard truly extraordinary stories about the power of books in the lives of children. In one case, a homeless child, who had been bounced from one location to another, later resurfaced—and the only possession that he had fought to keep was the book he was given as part of a First Book distribution months earlier. More recently, I met a child who, upon receiving the book he wanted, flashed a big smile and said, "This is my big chance!" These snapshots reveal the true power of books and stories to give hope and change lives.

As these children grow up and continue to develop their love of reading, they will owe a profound debt to those volunteers who reached out to them—a debt that they may repay by reaching out to spark the next generation of readers. But there is a greater debt owed by all of us—a debt to the storytellers, the authors, who have bound us together, inspired our leaders, fueled our civilizations, and helped us put our children to sleep with their heads full of images and ideas.

WHO WROTE THAT? is a series of books dedicated to introducing us to a few of these incredible individuals. While we have almost always honored stories, we have not uniformly honored storytellers. In fact, some of the most important authors have toiled in complete obscurity throughout their lives or have been openly persecuted for the uncomfortable truths that they have laid before us. When confronted with the magnitude of their written work or perhaps the daily grind of our own, we can forget that writers are people. They struggle through the same daily indignities and dental appointments, and they experience the intense joy and bottomless despair that many of us do. Yet somehow they rise above it all to deliver a powerful thread that connects us all. It is a rare honor to have the opportunity that these books provide to share the lives of these extraordinary people. Enjoy.

Lemony Snicket (Daniel Handler) gives a dramatic reading of The End, *the final book in* A Series of Unfortunate Events *at a Barnes & Noble bookstore in New York City in October 2006.*

1

Who Is Lemony Snicket?

WHILE LEMONY SNICKET is perhaps best known as the author of the 13 books that, to date, make up *A Series of Unfortunate Events*, his own life story (or what exactly is known of it) is equally fascinating in its own right.

Snicket, as readers of the series well know, is constantly on the run, falsely accused of crimes he has not committed, hunted both by the police and his enemies, and is the fire-starting side of the top-secret organization, the V.F.D. (The V.F.D. is the Volunteer Fire Department, an organization at war with itself. One half is made up of arsonists who start fires, the other half puts out the fires. The reasons for the split, however, are still unknown.)

Lemony Snicket is, or was, one of three siblings, all of whom were kidnapped and inducted into the V.F.D. Snicket attended a V.F.D.-run boarding school, where it seems likely that he first met Count Olaf, the notorious villain described in *A Series of Unfortunate Events*. After graduation, Snicket was employed by the newspaper *The Daily Punctilio* where he worked for a time as an obituary spell-checker, before being sent on a series of seemingly pointless missions and having all ties to his previous life severed.

It is also known that it was during this time that Snicket fell in love with actress Beatrice, a fellow member of the V.F.D. The two were engaged to be married, but for reasons that still remain unclear, Beatrice broke off the engagement and returned her ring—along with a 200-page book explaining in great detail why the couple could never marry—to Snicket.

That would have been enough to cause great unhappiness on its own, but after what can only be called a series of unfortunate events, Snicket found himself falsely accused of murder and arson, and began his life on the run. Beatrice recovered from her broken engagement and went on to marry Bertrand Baudelaire, thus becoming the mother of Violet, Klaus, and Sunny Baudelaire, the much put-upon young heroes of *A Series of Unfortunate Events*.

Years later, Beatrice and Bertrand Baudelaire were killed when their home was burned to the ground, leaving their children orphans, and beginning Violet, Klaus, and Sunny's *own* series of unfortunate events. Snicket, feeling that he owed as much to his one-time fiancée, set out to chronicle the lives of the Baudelaire children, at least until they came of age. As he revealed in a later interview with the publisher of *A Series of Unfortunate Events*, HarperCollins: "For various personal and legal reasons, I began researching the terrible things that happened to the three Baudelaire children following the death of their parents. The good people at HarperCollins offered to publish my findings, both as cautionary tales and for the general good."[1]

But although his books chronicling the adventures of the Baudelaire children make it clear that he knows a great deal about their lives, it seems unlikely that he himself has ever met any of them. There are those, however, who believe that Snicket is actually the taxi driver who appears in the books *The Penultimate Peril*, *The Reptile Room*, and *The Wide Window*. Indeed, it is this very same man who is thought to possess the sugar bowl, an important plot element of the series, after he recovered it from the pond where it was hidden.

Little else is known about Snicket's personal life. It is a matter of record that as a child his hobbies included taxidermy (the art of preparing, stuffing, and mounting the skins of dead animals so that they appear lifelike) and playing the harpsichord.

Today, he critically describes himself in no uncertain terms as a coward and makes it clear to all that he is not capable of being as brave as the Baudelaire children are. He has confessed that he did things in the past that he is not proud of, in particular the original theft of the sugar bowl from Esme Squalor. He has also hinted that he had some part in the murder of Count Olaf's parents, and that Beatrice was involved as well.

Finally, *The Daily Punctilio*, a newspaper never known for its accuracy, reported Mr. Snicket's death, as later reproduced in *Lemony Snicket: The Unauthorized Autobiography*, published in 2002:

> Lemony Snicket, author of *A Series of Unfortunate Events*, the purportedly true chronicles of the Baudelaire children, was reported dead today by anonymous and possibly unreliable sources. His age was given as "tall, with brown eyes." He leaves no known survivors.
>
> Born on a cattle farm rather than in a hospital, Snicket had a promising scholarly career, beginning with a job as a theatrical critic—in all senses of the word—for this very newspaper, followed by a series of several promising anthropomorphic treatises, a word which here means "very long reports." This period of professional contentment—and, allegedly, unrequited love—ended when news broke of his involvement with V.F.D. and the accompanying scandal was reported in these very pages.
>
> Mr. Snicket became a fugitive from justice and was rarely seen in public, and then usually from the back. Several manhunts—and, due to a typographical error, womanhunts—proved fruitless. At least the Baudelaire's story, and his, appears to be over.
>
> As no one seems to know when, where, how, and why he died, there will be no funeral services. A burial may be scheduled later this year.[2]

THE REAL LEMONY SNICKET

Of course, none of the above is exactly true. There really isn't a Lemony Snicket. There is, however, the actual person Daniel Handler, the creator of Lemony Snicket and author of *A Series of Unfortunate Events*. Like many authors, Handler chose to write the series using a pen name, or a *nom de plume*, as it is sometimes called. This allows Handler a certain amount of freedom: He can publish books for adults under his own name, while publishing children's books using the name Lemony Snicket.

(It also means, of course, that when fans go a bookstore reading to meet Lemony Snicket, they are greeted by his representative, a man named Daniel Handler. Handler will then politely apologize for Mr. Snicket's absence and entertain the fans himself, perhaps even, if they are lucky, busting out his accordion!)

There are, of course, many authors who write using a pen name. Samuel Clemens is best known by his pen name, Mark Twain. Charles Dodgson used the pen name Lewis Carroll when writing books such as *Alice's Adventures in Wonderland*. Even modern writers sometimes use a pen name: Stephen King has written several books using the name Richard Bachman because his publishers were afraid that he was writing too many books under his real name.

But unlike those other writers, Daniel Handler did not just create the name Lemony Snicket. He made him a character in his own right, as not only the narrator of *A Series of Unfortunate Events* but also as a man with his own life story. Indeed, Handler often seems content to remain hidden behind Lemony Snicket. And, truth be told, how many of you, up until just a few paragraphs ago, thought that the books actually *were* written by a man named Lemony Snicket?

So who then is Daniel Handler? He is the author of more than 23 books, including the 13 novels in *A Series of Unfortunate Events* and three novels for adults written under his own name. He is a highly respected editor and contributor who has written the introductions to such classic American novels as Herman Melville's *The Confidence Man* under his own name, and, under the name of Lemony Snicket, a hilarious introduction to the story *Noisy Outlaws, Unfriendly Blobs, and Some Other Things That Aren't as Scary, Maybe, Depending on How You Feel About Lost Lands, Stray Cellphones, Creatures from the Sky, Parents who Disappear in Peru, a Man Named Lars Farf, and One Other Story We Couldn't Quite Finish, So Maybe you Could Help Us Out.*

He has written the text for a classical music piece for orchestra entitled *The Composer Is Dead* and has served as its narrator. He has written screenplays for three movies. He has played accordion on the three-album set *69 Love Songs* by The Magnetic Fields. He is a political activist and one of the founders of the group LitPAC. He is, obviously, a man of many hats and interests.

How did he do it? How did Daniel Handler become Lemony Snicket and create a series of children's books that has sold more than 55 million copies worldwide and been published in more than 40 different languages? How did a man whose personal philosophy as Lemony Snicket is "Never refuse a breath mint" go on to become one of the most beloved children's authors of our time? His story begins in San Francisco, and involves opera, accounting, and the desire to be a dark and mysterious person.

A young Daniel Handler learned to appreciate opera from his parents. Here soprano Elina Garanca (as Carmen) and tenor Roberto Alagna (as Don Jose) perform in director Richard Eyre's production of George Bizet's Carmen *at the Metropolitan Opera in New York City on December 28, 2009.*

Childhood

COMPARED TO THE fictional Lemony Snicket, Daniel Handler had what can only be described as a normal childhood. Or, as normal as anyone's childhood can truly be. He was born on February 28, 1970, in San Francisco, California. His mother, Sandra Handler, was the dean of behavioral sciences at the City College of San Francisco. His father, Lou Handler, was a certified public accountant. He has one younger sister, Rebecca.

Growing up, Handler had two abiding loves: music and books. His love of music came, at least in part, from his mother, who, along with her duties at City College, was also an opera singer. Indeed, it was at the opera that his parents met.

Handler jokingly writes on Lemony Snicket's Web site, "My mother was playing Aida, and she remains to this day the hippest white woman in San Francisco."[1] (And while it is true that she never starred in the opera "Aida," it is at least possible that she is the hippest white woman living in San Francisco.)

Like many children, Handler took piano lessons when he was young. But unlike many children, when he entered high school he also learned to play two rather unusual musical instruments: the tuba and the accordion. Since neither of these is the usual choice of instruments, it should be obvious that even at that age, Daniel Handler was not your average kid. You may be wondering why, in particular, Handler wanted to learn how to play the accordion. He has been quoted as saying he learned it "to drive his parents crazy!" Indeed, Handler said in an interview that when he told his parents of his decision they reacted "as if I had taken up heroin."[2] (Heroin is a highly addictive drug that is very bad for you, and undoubtedly, something his parents would not have been at all happy about his using.)

The young Daniel Handler also inherited from his parents a love of opera, and sang with the San Francisco Boys Chorus in the early 1980s in productions of *La Boheme*, *Carmen*, *Tosca*, and many others. In a joke that the grown-up Daniel Handler (or Lemony Snicket) would appreciate, his parents used to tease that "they considered castration to elongate"[3] his singing career. His opera career came to an end, but his love of opera never ended. He remains a fan of opera, loving its narrative style; in fact, he structured his second adult novel, *Watch Your Mouth*, as an opera.

His other great love growing up was for books, a love supported by his parents, who were both voracious readers. They read to him and encouraged him to read on his own. One of their tricks to keep him interested in reading is one that he uses when writing his own books today. He recalled:

> One thing that they did I just thought was fantastic was that they would read to me when I was very young and stop at a suspenseful moment. And then they would say, "Well, it's now time for bed. And, you know, under no circumstances should you read with this light over here that we're placing near your bed. Under no circumstances should you turn this on and read it." And then, of course, I would. And then the next day when the bookmark was in a different place in the book, they would read it as if nothing had happened. And that, to me, seemed particularly effective. And perhaps that's the root of Mr. Snicket's—"Don't read this book. You'll only end up in bad trouble."[4]

His choice of books once again proved Handler's slightly different take on life. Unlike many young readers, he disliked any children's books with predictable endings. And, if he happened to read a book with a happy ending and all the characters living happily ever after, he would throw it aside, angry at himself that he had wasted his time reading it.

Not only did he want the books he read not to end well, he wanted to read books in which the characters had scary things happen to them—characters who lived through, as it were, a series of unfortunate events. Handler elaborated on this in a 2000 interview with *Publishers Weekly*:

> I have always preferred stories in which mysterious and creepy things happen. As a kid, I hated books where everyone joined the softball team and had a grand time or found true love on a picnic. I liked stories set in an eerie castle that was invaded by a snake that strangled the residents.[5]

Is it any wonder, then, that the very first words in the very first book in *A Series of Unfortunate Events* are the

One of the great influences on A Series of Unfortunate Events *was the work of the author and illustrator Edward Gorey, who died at age 75 on April 15, 2000. Here, Gorey gives an interview in April 1994 at his home in Cape Cod, Massachusetts. He illustrated 60 books, designed sets for stage productions, including Broadway's* Dracula, *and wrote at least 90 books.*

following: "If you are interested in stories with happy endings, you would be better off reading some other book. In this book, not only is there no happy ending, there is no happy beginning and very few happy things in the middle."[6]

Despite his strong list of likes and dislikes, Handler did manage to find several authors whose books pleased him to no end. One of his favorite authors growing up was Roald Dahl, whose books for children such as *The Witches, Fantastic Mr. Fox*, and *Charlie and the Chocolate Factory* are known for their scary dark humor. He was also a fan of the writer Zilpha Keatley Snyder,

> who is not . . . well-known, but is just a terrific writer. She wrote *The Egypt Game* and *The Headless Cupid* and a bunch of really interesting books where children are forced to negotiate difficult but not super-natural circumstances more or less all by themselves, and those were the sort of stories that appealed to me.[7]

DISCOVERING EDWARD GOREY

Perhaps Handler's favorite author—whose influence can be clearly seen in Handler's own books—was Edward Gorey, known for his humorously macabre illustrated books. Indeed, the very first book that Daniel Handler bought with his own money was Gorey's *The Blue Aspic*. A description of the book posted on Amazon.com leaves little doubt that anyone will be surprised at Handler's choice:

> Ortenzia Caviglia is an undiscovered opera understudy whose lucky break results from the mysterious murder of the reigning diva. Upon hearing her sing, Jasper Ankle becomes her deepest admirer, undaunted by perilous weather and abject poverty in his quest to hear her sing. As Ortenzia's star rises, Jasper sinks further into despair, until performer and fan collide in true Edward Gorey fashion. Exquisitely illustrated with

Gorey's signature pen-and-ink crosshatching, *The Blue Aspic* is a heart-wrenching and oddly hilarious tale of unrequited love and the dangers of celebrity.[8]

Gorey's work, not unlike Handler's, has been called gothic, a word which here means a literary style composed of fantastic tales dealing with horror, despair, and other dark subjects that became popular during the late eighteenth and early nineteenth centuries. Gorey, on the other hand, preferred to call his work "literary nonsense," here meaning a style made famous by writers such as Lewis Carroll and Edward Lear. But when asked about his decision to write "gothic" literature, Gorey defended his style in words that would have made the young Daniel Handler very happy:

> If you're doing nonsense it has to be rather awful, because there'd be no point. I'm trying to think if there's sunny nonsense. Sunny, funny nonsense for children—oh, how boring,

Did you know...

Daniel Handler thinks he may have killed Edward Gorey. After Handler had completed the first two books in *A Series of Unfortunate Events*—*The Bad Beginning* and *The Reptile Room*—he sent copies to his idol, Edward Gorey, along with a note saying that he hoped that he would be forgiven for everything he had stolen from Gorey's works (which is, to be honest, quite a lot). Gorey died just a few weeks later. Coincidence? Handler said in an interview that he likes to think that he killed him but, of course, has no proof that he actually did.

boring, boring. As Schubert said, there is no happy music. And that's true, there really isn't. And there's probably no happy nonsense, either.[9]

Handler claims to have come by his gothic sensibility "with childhood viewings of *Nosferatu* and teenage obsessions with Ann Radcliffe and The Cure, and I enjoy a good Wilkie Collins novel to this day."[10] These influences are very different, but they are also quite dark. *Nosferatu* is a silent film version of the Dracula story directed by the great German director F.W. Murnau. Ann Radcliffe was a gothic novelist whose most famous work, *The Mysteries of Udolpho*, tells the story of Emily St. Aubert, who, over the course of the novel, suffers the death of her father, supernatural terrors in a remarkably gloomy castle, and the plotting of an Italian scoundrel named Montoni. The Cure, an English rock band led by Robert Smith, is perhaps the definitive "goth" band. And finally, Wilkie Collins is a nineteenth-century English novelist who wrote what were called at the time "sensation novels" and which are seen today as the first detective and suspense fiction.

HIS FAVORITE BOOK

As much as Handler loved the works of Dahl and Gorey, his favorite book while he was growing up is a book you have probably never even heard of. An Italian novel first published in 1945, it is *The Bears' Famous Invasion of Sicily*, written and illustrated by Dino Buzzati.

The book describes a horrible winter in Sicily, one so horrible that the bears are forced to leave their mountain home to go down into the valley to find food. There, they struggle against an army of wild boars, crafty professors who may (or may not) be magicians, the snarling Marmoset the Cat, and possible treachery within their own ranks. Despite it all, the bears triumph.

Handler loved and remembered the book for so long that when he became a successful author, he persuaded a publisher, the New York Review Children's Collection, to reissue the book, which had gone out of print. Not only that, but for the paperback edition of the book, Lemony Snicket wrote both an introduction and reader's guide, providing interesting questions at the end of each chapter.

Obviously, the book meant and still does mean a lot to Handler. He wrote a love letter to the book that was published on the back cover of the reissue:

> *The Bears' Famous Invasion of Sicily* is one of the noblest books I know. At once a tragic history and a philosophical inquiry, the novel examines ambition, violence, and revenge in the voice of an adult explaining things to children—a voice that is simultaneously wise, wry, and wrong. Little wonder that it's not only my favorite book, but Lemony Snicket's as well.[11]

Printed directly below that on the back cover is the exact same letter, with the following change in the last sentence: "Little wonder that it is not only my favorite book, but Daniel Handler's as well."[12] In other words, *The Bears' Famous Invasion of Sicily* is not only Daniel Handler's favorite book; it's his fictional character Lemony Snicket's favorite book as well.

There is one other favorite book of young Daniel Handler's that helped point him in the direction of eventually becoming a writer himself. He recalled:

> I read Carson McCullers's *Ballad of the Sad Café* when I was in eighth grade. I already wanted to be a writer but it occurred to me for the first time that I might learn how to do this by re-reading books I loved and figuring out how they were made.

I took extensive notes on the McCullers, which is pretty much how I do it today.[13]

AN AWARENESS OF TERRIBLE THINGS

It should be obvious by now that the opera singing, accordion playing, unhappy-ending reading Daniel Handler was not your typical young American boy. To top it all off, he was not particularly interested in sports, and often let the ball get past him on the soccer field because he was more interested in looking at insects. So, not surprisingly, he did not like reading the usual boy's books about sports. In an interview, he told Terry Gross of National Public Radio (NPR):

> I think it's always depressing to me that there's so many books marketed for young boys who want to read that are about sports. I mean, I was always—I could never play any sports and I always wanted to go away and read a book. And to be offered a book in which boys played sports seemed to be the very opposite of what I wanted.[14]

Instead of wanting to read about sports and sports heroes, Handler grew up with an intense awareness of the fact that sometimes, despite everyone's best efforts, terrible things can happen to children. This worldview came about during Handler's childhood. His Jewish father, Lou Handler, had fled with his family from Nazi Germany while still a child. As a young boy, Daniel grew up knowing that the Nazis had attempted to systematically exterminate European Jews in the Holocaust. How could that not affect him?

Which is not necessarily to say that Handler grew up in an observant Jewish home. As he described it in an interview with *Moment* magazine:

> Observant is sort of a comparative term. We didn't have a kosher kitchen. It was a sort of typical Jewish household

that hovered between Reform and Conservative Judaism. All major holidays and rituals were kept up but we occasionally lapsed on Sukkot and could never remember what Sh'imini Atzeret was for.[15]

Of the three major branches of Judaism, Reform Judaism is the most relaxed in its enforcement of Jewish laws, Conservative is in the middle, and Orthodox is the most strict. Sukkot, the feast of tabernacles, is considered a major Jewish holiday. Sh'imini Atzeret, although often thought of as being the eighth day of the festival of Sukkot, is actually a holiday in and of itself.

Handler may not have known much about his religion while he was growing up, but his knowledge of the Holocaust and of the evil of which mankind is capable contributed to his childhood sense that the world of adults could be a little scary. Handler said:

> I think I had a sense that the world was not in my control, that decisions were being made on my behalf by people much taller than me who were unlikely to pay attention no matter how many times I repeated my question. And I think I'm not alone in that perception, and that's why there's so many evil and/or inept adults in my books.[16]

So, to sum up, Daniel Handler was an opera-singing, book-reading, non-sports playing, accordion-toting young man. He was, at least on the face of it, not a likely candidate to be particularly popular. Yet he was. As he said in a later interview, "I was the sort of kid that was funny enough that I wouldn't get beat up."[17] Like many a young person who was considered "different," he used humor as a way to make himself liked.

But behind the humor, there was always a serious young man. As he told Sally Lodge of *Publishers Weekly*,

"I always wanted to be a dark, mysterious person; instead I was a bright and obvious person."[18] It is the combination of those two halves of his personality—the humorous and the dark—that make *A Series of Unfortunate Events* such an unforgettable reading experience.

Handler also knew from an early age that, one way or another, he was going to be a writer. As he told one interviewer:

> I could never think of anything else that I wanted to be. My parents tell a story that when I was five years old I said I wanted to be a philosopher that lived on top of a hill and would give out advice to anybody who climbed up there. I don't have a memory of that but if so that was the only other career I ever considered.[19]

HIGH SCHOOL AND BEYOND

In San Francisco, Handler attended the prestigious Lowell High School, the oldest public high school west of the Mississippi River in the continental United States. It is considered to be one of the best and most demanding high schools in the country. Handler graduated at the top of his class and tied for the highly sought after award for "Best Personality." According to one former classmate, he was also voted "Class Clown," "Best Actor," "Chatterbox," and "Teacher's Pet."

Handler would revisit his time at Lowell High School 11 years later by setting his first novel, *The Basic Eight*, in Roewer High School, a school where students are "pushed to the limits academically, socially and athletically."[20] But that would be years in the future. Like many high school students, Handler picked a college as far away from home as possible. So in 1988, Handler left San Francisco and moved to Connecticut to attend Wesleyan University. It turned out to be a major move, both on an academic and on a personal level.

Daniel Handler's interest in writing first blossomed at Wesleyan University in Middletown, Connecticut, where his poetry won awards. Here, Senator Barack Obama of Illinois speaks at the school's commencement on May 25, 2008, during that year's presidential campaign.

Becoming a Poet

HANDLER LEFT SAN FRANCISCO in the fall of 1988, moving to Middletown, Connecticut to attend Wesleyan University. Wesley, the first institute of higher learning to be named after John Wesleyan, the founder of Methodism, was established in 1831 and is today considered to be one of the nation's most highly ranked colleges.

Handler attended Wesleyan for four years, studying writing with Kit Reed and examining the works of such noted writers as Vladimir Nabokov with Priscilla Meyer, and earned a Bachelor of Arts degree in American studies. All three, the professors Reed and Meyer, and the Russian writer Nabokov, had an enormous influence on Handler, teaching him a simple lesson: "The way to become a good writer is to write."[1]

While there, he met and began dating an aspiring graphic designer and illustrator named Lisa Brown. He also decided on what kind of writer he wanted to be. Throughout his time at Lowell High School, he had written poetry, some of which had been published in the school's literary magazine. Years later, Handler went back to reread some of what he had written.

> I actually visited my high school literary magazine . . . and they found some of my old poetry on file and [had] given it to me. And it was pretty interesting to read. It was lousy of course. But I felt like it still had some respectability to it.
>
> It was two poems I had written . . . about love and sex. And so of course they're mortifying. But they have an air of detachment, I guess, and one of them rhymes. And it's interesting to me that I was already trying to find an acceptable format for perhaps embarrassing ideas.[2]

But now that he was in college, the already serious young man started taking his poetry writing much more seriously. He recalled:

> By the time I was in college, I was writing a lot of poetry that was being published in tiny journals and was winning little student prizes and things like that. And I think that was probably the first time I began to think of myself as a writer who was producing work that was of merit, at least for the age I was.[3]

In this interview, Handler is just being modest. He received more than just "little student prizes and things like that." He won an award from the Academy of American

During his time at Wesleyan University, Daniel Handler was influenced by a number of important authors, most notably the twentieth-century Russian émigré Vladimir Nabokov, who is best known for such novels as Lolita, *first published in 1955, and* Pale Fire, *first published in 1962.*

Poets in 1990 and went on tour as a Connecticut Student Poet. It was, without a doubt, a promising start for the career of the young aspiring poet. But something was beginning to happen to his writing that steered him away from poetry and into another direction entirely:

> When I was in college, my poems started getting longer and longer and more and more narrative. And I have a very clear memory of talking to a poetry professor of mine who finally said to me very gently that there was actually a tradition of long, non-line-based narrative poetry called "prose." And it was like he just took me across the hallway or something [and

Did you know...

Although his writing developed, and Daniel Handler went from being a poet to a writer of prose, he still loves poetry. In an interview with Barnes and Noble, he listed some of his favorite books, one of which is *The Complete Poems 1927–1979* by Elizabeth Bishop, one of America's greatest poets. He remarked: "Everyone should read more poetry. It's not hard. Just purchase this book and keep it on your bed-stand and read one poem every couple of days and watch your life get better."*

So do what Daniel Handler suggests—read more poetry!

*"Meet the Writers," http://www.barnesandnoble. com/writers/writerdetails.asp?cid=968086# interview.

said] "There is this thing you can do in which you don't have to worry that your sentences are long and you seem to be telling a story."[4]

In other words, Handler's writing was growing beyond the confines of poetry. If his writing was naturally moving in that direction, he would have no choice but to follow his voice and work on writing short stories and novels. (You will no doubt be relieved to know, though, that Handler still writes the occasional poem, but he says, "I don't do anything with it.")[5]

So, armed with his degree in American Studies and the need to become a writer, Handler remained in Middletown and set out to work. He had received an Olin Fellowship when he graduated Wesleyan, so his financial needs were at least partially met, but he still had fears of failure as well as the stigma of remaining in his college town after graduating. He recalled the period in an interview:

> I was writing a novel in a basement apartment that I'd finagled for free on campus the year after graduating. And I had a small grant and a job playing piano for modern dance classes. And although I was fairly happy (one of the reasons I had stayed on for another year is that my then-girlfriend, now-wife was a year behind me in school), it was a very self-conscious position to be in because there was so much of it that stank of being a loser—that I was still in Middletown, Connecticut, the year after I graduated. And I was afraid I was one of those guys—there were always a few of those guys who would keep on going to college parties for years afterward. So even though no one was reading the work that I was doing, I felt a great sense of sort of overcoming the personal stigma of what I was doing.[6]

STRUGGLES AND MARRIAGE

That first attempt at writing a novel—like many other such attempts written by other would-be authors—ended up in the wastebasket after several stabs at revision. (Although that may not be entirely true. That work, was, according to Handler, "a mock-gothic story entitled 'A Series Of Unfortunate Events' and the sharp-eyed reader will discern that it was not entirely discarded."[7]) He would just have to start all over again. But the grant money had run out, so he was forced to work a number of odd jobs, some of which he listed in a 2003 interview with *Redivider*: "Bookstore employee, cocktail pianist, cater waiter, bartender, dance accompanist, something roughly approximating a butler, Kafkaesque administrative position, radio script writer, movie reviewer, manuscript summarizer, freelance complainer."[8]

Of these, perhaps the most interesting job, at least in terms of Handler's future success as an author (outside of freelance complainer), was writing comedy sketches for a nationally syndicated radio show based in his hometown of San Francisco, "The House of Blues Radio Hour." But no matter what job he had, he kept working on his novel, writing and rewriting it until he was happy enough with it to try to find a publisher willing to publish it. This, however, proved far easier said then done. Perhaps, he thought, a change of location was what he (and his manuscript) needed. A change of place might help change his luck as well.

As a struggling writer, Daniel Handler moved to New York City to make a name for himself. Seen here, the vibrant street life and outdoor cafes of the New York neighborhood of SoHo.

4

A Change
of Location
and Direction

DANIEL HANDLER MOVED to New York City, where, in
1998, he married his long-time girlfriend Lisa Brown, and completed a second novel, *Watch Your Mouth*. At the same time,
though, his first novel, *The Basic Eight*, was still in the process
of being rejected. Thirty-seven publishers in all, according to
Handler, looked at it and said, basically, "No, thank you." Imagine it: You are a young writer, newly married, and publisher
after publisher keeps telling you that your work is not good
enough for them to publish. Handler recalled:

> I told myself, over and over, that the depressing tumult in which
> I was living would be regarded, in the rosy prism of memory, as

short-lived, bohemian and even somewhat glamorous, and I was more or less right. Of course, I had the advantages of beginning my career during a recession, so every last one of my peers was also failing and flailing, and of living near a very cheap taqueria with very strong drinks.[1]

Finally though, Handler had the breakthrough he had been looking for. His first novel, which had taken six long years to write and had been rejected 37 times, had "finally sold for the smallest amount of money my literary agent had ever negotiated for a work of fiction."[2] For Handler, though, the money, while important, did not quite matter. He was going to be a published author. Now his fate would be up to the critics, and, even more importantly, to the readers—if, of course, there were any.

THE BASIC EIGHT GETS PUBLISHED

It is one of the proudest moments of a young writer's life. For Handler, who had struggled so hard to get his book published, the moment his book was sold seemed, literally, unbelievable:

> It seemed like possibly a hoax. I had written the first draft of *Watch Your Mouth* while waiting for *The Basic Eight* to be sold, so I had two unsold novels that I was dragging around with me, and they were feeling like cement shoes. It was bad enough to have one, but to have two . . . My chances for survival felt about nil.[3]

But it was no hoax. The year 1999 saw the publication of Daniel Handler's first novel, *The Basic Eight*. Like many first novels, *The Basic Eight* is partially autobiographical. The book focuses on a group of high school students in a clique, who call themselves The Basic Eight.

The school, Roewer High, is obviously based on Handler's alma mater, Lowell High School. And, as Handler said in an interview with Philana Woo in Lowell's school paper, *The Lowell*, the school's fictional name is in itself a cruel joke:

> When I was at Lowell, it was called Roewer . . . Lowell then
> was predominantly Asian . . . and Roewer was the name people
> of all races referred to it. It was sort of the kids' joke about the
> fact that most of the school was Asian. I guess Roewer could
> be an offensive way of making a pun on an Asian accent.[4]

Cruel indeed. But then, cruelty is the name of the game at Roewer. As one interviewer described the book, "As an examination of some very topical '90s themes—high school cliques, absinthe abuse, high school violence, Oprah Winfrey—*The Basic Eight* is unmatched for its interplay of sensitive humor and outright cool."[5]

The book begins at the end of the action. The story is narrated by Flannery Culp, who tells of the, well, series of unfortunate events that took place in her senior year, based on the entries in her journal. Culp is relating the story from prison, where she is serving time for the murder of a teacher and fellow student. Angry at the way she has been treated in the press (which had called her the leader of a Satanic cult), Flannery attempts to set the record straight about what actually happened that year at Roewer.

Although smart, funny, and editor of the school paper, Culp has problems in calculus and relies on seven friends for support: "Queen Bee" Kate; Natasha, whom Flan admires; Gabriel, a black student and chef who is in love with Flan; Douglas, who introduced absinthe (an alcoholic drink reputed to have the power to cause visions) to the group; V, a girl whose name is kept secret to provide anonymity to her famous family; Lily; and the beautiful Jennifer Rose Milton.

The friends go to class together, skip class together, drink coffee together, plan dinner parties together, drink alcohol together, listen to classical and alternative music together, and attend the Grand Opera Breakfast Club together. But when Douglas introduces absinthe into the mix, things quickly go out of control, as when Natasha rescues Flan by poisoning a biology teacher who has been making her life difficult, and when Adam State, whom Flan loves but who is in love with Kate, becomes a victim of Flan's jealousy and is murdered with a croquet mallet.

The Basic Eight is, at its heart, a coming-of-age novel, whose teenage characters, seemingly left to their own devices, ape the adult world around them by throwing extravagant dinner parties and drinking from hip flasks. Of the novel, a reviewer for *Publishers Weekly* wrote, "The links between teen social life, tabloid culture and serious violence have been explored below and exploited before, but Handler, and Flannery, know that, if they're not the first to use such material, they may well be the coolest."[6] The reviewer concluded by adding "Handler's confident satire is not only cheeky but packed with downright lovable characters whose youthful misadventures keep the novel neatly balanced between absurdity and poignancy."[7]

A book whose heroine kills the boy she loves with a croquet mallet features "lovable" characters? The reviewer for *Booklist* may have come closer to the mark with her description of the book as "Part horror story, part black comedy," noting that the book shows what can happen to "smart, privileged, cynical teens with too few rules, too much to drink, too little supervision, and boundless imagination."[8]

A lithograph of Othello, Desdemona, and Iago during the handkerchief scene in William Shakespeare's tragedy Othello, the Moor of Venice. *Believed to have been first written in 1603, the play is referenced in a number of ways in Daniel Handler's novel,* The Basic Eight.

Although the majority of the reviews were favorable, some reviewers objected to the book's uneasy mixture of murder and social satire. "Handler is a charming writer with a lovely mastery of voice," wrote one reviewer, "but the book is weakened by his attempt to turn a clever idea into a social satire."[9] While Brian Howard, writing in Citypaper.net added that "the oh-my-gosh plot twist, which ultimately ruins Culp's credibility, also does much to undo Handler's otherwise fine debut."[10]

The Basic Eight is, indeed, a fine first book. In it, Handler shows early on his ability to handle a narrative, to allow the narrator's voice to be an important part of the storytelling process, and to combine, if somewhat uneasily, humor and horror. He also displayed some of the narrative tricks that would soon become trademark Handler (or is it Snicket?) traits.

For example, the narrator in *A Series of Unfortunate Events* takes the time to define what certain words mean in the context of the text; in *The Basic Eight* Flan breaks up the story with the inclusion of study guides every few pages, both mocking literary criticism and giving the reader something to ponder. Handler also generously fills the book with literary allusions. For example, Shakespeare's tragedy of jealousy gone wild, *Othello*, is referred to in ways both obvious (the student play for the year is *Othello*) and more subtle (a handkerchief, which plays an important part in *Othello*, also plays a part in *The Basic Eight*).

The author, who was happy with the way the novel turned out, described the book's theme as being "that young people are oftentimes full of great ideas and creativity and that those things are often stifled."[11] The book's sales benefited from the fact that it hit the shelves just one month after the Columbine High School tragedy had focused the nation's attention on violence among teenagers.

The book, while relatively successful for a first novel, did not make Handler a household name, and despite being a published author, he still kept working a series of part-time jobs to help pay the bills. Years later, Handler was asked what he would have done to support himself if the best he had been able to do as a writer in terms of sales was *The Basic Eight*. He replied:

> It is quite easy to imagine myself without the benefit of the Snicket books, because I'd be in the same boat as nearly every other writer I know—teaching, freelancing, the occasional grant. I always assumed that I'd end up teaching someplace, and it's still a career I find interesting.[2]

His second adult novel, *Watch Your Mouth*, the one he had been dragging around at the same time as *The Basic Eight*, came out in 2000. Another coming-of-age novel, it tells the story of the summer the main character Joseph

Did you know...

What's an average day like for Daniel Handler? Pretty simple actually. He claims he wakes up early, scowls at the newspaper while drinking his coffee and grapefruit juice, works at his desk until late afternoon with very few breaks, takes a walk and buys some groceries, comes back to his desk and scowls at what he has written that day, returns only the phone calls he feels he must, reads and sips a refreshing cocktail, cooks and eats dinner (made with the very same groceries he purchased earlier), watches old movies that he has rented from a neighborhood establishment, and reads some more.

Not exactly a glamorous life, is it?

spent with his Jewish girlfriend, Cynthia Glass, in her hometown of Pittsburgh, Pennsylvania.

Interestingly, the first part of *Watch Your Mouth* is laid out as an opera. Instead of chapter titles, there are act and scene numbers, and each of the characters is assigned a singing voice. As the summer progresses, Joseph begins to realize that the Glass family is engaging in what can only be called inappropriate behavior, while at the same time Cynthia's mother, Mimi, seems to be building a golem in her basement. (A golem is a creature from Jewish folklore, a living being made entirely of nonliving matter such as mud or clay.) The first part of the book ends, as do most operas, in death.

The second part of the novel is slightly more conventional. Joseph attempts to recover from the events of the first part of the novel. This part is told in the form of a 12-step program—a program based on a set of principles, usually 12 in number, used to recover from a behavioral problem such as alcoholism or compulsive behavior. When asked why he chose such an unconventional format (or formats) for his second novel, Handler replied:

> I've always been a fan of opera. I've always liked its sense of narrative. It's contained, because it has to take place in one room or one town, yet it's always absurdly melodramatic. And with family, you're trapped in the same house with a few people, and the allegiances are changing every five minutes. So family and opera seemed to go together.
>
> So many novels about families just *end*, as if family stories could just end. "And then they had a revelation, and everybody realized they could do this." And I've never seen that happen in any family, so I liked the idea of extending a novel past what seemed like the end of the story. And [after] the first half . . .

I asked myself what would happen if you'd been through such an experience, and, you know, you'd enter a 12-step program. And those programs seem to be all about placing a very strict narrative on a difficult and muddled experience. So that just seemed to fit very well, too.[13]

Watch Your Mouth received decidedly mixed reviews. Some critics felt it crossed the bounds of good taste. Many, however, praised Handler's humor and innovative style, with *Salon*'s Edward Neuert writing that Handler "is more than ready to pick up the torch of [Kurt Vonnegut] and write the kind of deftly funny absurdist story that both horrifies with its subject matter and hooks you with its humor." He added that there are "plays within plays and puns within puns . . . *Mouth* is clever, witty, and unpredictable."[14]

Despite its shocking subject manner and experimental style, the book, somewhat surprisingly, became a national bestseller in 2000. But not necessarily for the reasons you may think. Upon the advice of a children's book editor who had rejected *The Basic Eight*, Handler had written and published the first two novels in a little series of books that came to be known as *A Series of Unfortunate Events* in 1999. With their immediate success, Handler's other books became bestsellers as well. The man who said he "always thought I would be a very, very, minor but perhaps well-thought-of writer," was about to become very well known indeed.

A scene from Lemony Snicket's A Series of Unfortunate Events *(2004), directed by Brad Silberling. Shown here from left are Jim Carrey, as Count Olaf; Liam Aiken, as Klaus Baudelaire; one of the twins, Kara or Shelby Hoffman, as baby Sunny Baudelaire; and Emily Browning, as Violet Baudelaire.*

5

The Birth
of Lemony Snicket

THE BAD BEGINNING, the first of 13 novels in Lemony Snicket's *A Series of Unfortunate Events*, memorably begins:

If you are interested in stories with happy endings, you would be better off reading some other book. In this book, not only is there no happy ending, there is no happy beginning and very few happy things in the middle. This is because not very many happy things happened in the lives of the three Baudelaire youngsters. Violet, Klaus, and Sunny Baudelaire were intelligent children, and they were resourceful, and had pleasant facial features, but they were extremely unlucky, and most everything that happened to them was rife with misfortune, misery, and despair. I'm sorry to tell you this, but that is how the story goes.[1]

And with this introduction, we come to what is perhaps the most interesting part of our story, at least from the perspective of a young or young adult reader: the creation of Lemony Snicket and *A Series of Unfortunate Events*. Where did the idea come from? And perhaps most importantly: Where did the name Lemony Snicket come from?

The series started, curiously enough, with the manuscript for Handler's tale of a croquet mallet-wielding murderess, *The Basic Eight*. The author explained the connection in an interview he gave in 2005:

> I'd written my first novel for adults, which was called *The Basic Eight* and was set in a high school, and we were having a devil of a time selling it. It ended up in the hands of an editor of a children's publishing house, for which it was *entirely* inappropriate. She said, "Well, we can't publish this, but I think you should write something for children," which I thought was a really terrible idea. She kept pestering me, saying, "I think you'd be great to write for children," and "I'm looking for new writers." I was so broke and so desperate that I couldn't believe I was turning away an editor who was interested in my work, but I honestly thought that there was no way a children's publishing house would take any interest in my book.[2]

It is interesting to note that Daniel Handler, who is one of the most successful children's book authors working today, was absolutely convinced that no publisher would be interested in any children's book he might write. As he said in an interview with About.com, "I thought that would be a terrible idea, that the sort of stuff I would come up with would be completely inappropriate for a children's publishing house."[3] Fortunately for Handler, he had been lucky enough into finding an editor and publisher who "got" what he wanted to do. He recalled:

> And so, to get her off my back as much as anything else, I agreed to meet her in a bar to discuss an idea I had, because I figured she would say it was a really lousy idea. So if we were meeting in her office, it would be really awkward, but if we were meeting in a bar, then at least we would both have a drink in our hands. And I told her I had an idea for a gothic novel, which had been falling apart as I was writing it [Remember his abandoned *first* first novel, *A Series of Unfortunate Events*?], but I thought instead it could be the story of children growing through all these terrible things. I expected she would hate that idea, and instead she said she *liked* it, which embarrassed me even more, because I just thought it meant she was a lightweight. . . . I wrote some of the book and gave it to her, and I kept being amazed that people weren't horrified by it. I kept waiting for someone to say, "What is anyone thinking? We're not going to publish this," but they didn't, and the books were published.[4]

It is easy, of course, to understand Handler's feelings. First of all, on the face of it, this is a series of books about how "Three young siblings—handsome, clever and rich—lose their loving parents in a fire that destroys their mansion. . . . It gets worse."[5]

And there's one other factor to consider. When Handler first discussed the possibility of writing *A Series of Unfortunate Events*, children's book publishing was very different than it is today, with publishers rarely willing to take a chance on anything that could be considered risky, new, different, or cutting edge. But with the publication of J.K. Rowling's first Harry Potter book, *Harry Potter and the*

Sorcerer's Stone in the fall of 1998, the popularity of children's books, and of fantastical tales in particular, took off.

So thanks to a perceptive editor, Handler was ready to reap the benefits of an increased interest in children's literature. That editor, Susan Rich, told *Publishers Weekly* exactly what it was that attracted her to Handler's work:

> I greatly admired his writing for adults and decided to try to lure him over to our side—the children's side. I knew we shared a similar sensibility about children's books, which I'd define as a resistance to fall into the overly trodden paths of traditional stories, and which I'd define as a resistance to anything that is too sweet or patronizing or moralistic. . . . And so our discussion turned to the Baudelaire orphans.[6]

HOW TO SELL THE UNSELLABLE

Handler, a fairly quick writer, soon completed the first two books in the series. The publisher loved the books, but turned to Handler to figure out a way to market or sell the books. What could they do to make the books stand out, to make readers who had never heard of the books want to read them? For a while, Handler could not answer these questions. He recalled:

> [I]t took forever. I couldn't think of a thing to say. I looked at the other children's books that were full of giddy praise and corny rhetorical questions, you know, "Will she have a better time at summer camp than she thinks?" "How will she escape from the troll's dungeon?" All these terrible, terrible summaries of books, and I just couldn't . . . I was so convinced that the books were going to fail that I couldn't imagine how I could write something on the back that would drive people to them. Then I was in a pharmacy and I saw the warnings on the backs of poisonous substances, and I thought, "Well, *that's*

what I can do." So I wrote a list of ingredients in the book, and warnings that they shouldn't consume those ingredients. The editor and the publisher thought that it was a great way to go in terms of reverse psychology, but it honestly hadn't occurred to me that it was reverse psychology. I just thought that it was a sort of an honest assessment making clear that if you were timid or easily disturbed, you could turn away.[7]

(What, you might be asking yourself, is reverse psychology? Let us say, for example, that your parents have prepared an especially delicious dish of brussels sprouts for your dinner. If they told you directly to try it, you probably would say no. But if, instead, they told you that you probably would not like it, that it was a dish just for adults, you might be tempted to try it. That is reverse psychology.)

So, just in case you do not have your copy of *The Bad Beginning* handy, what exactly did Daniel Handler write on the back cover to "drive people to these books?"

Dear Reader,

I'm sorry to say that the book you are holding in your hands is extremely unpleasant. It tells an unhappy tale about three very unlucky children. Even though they are charming and clever, the Baudelaire siblings lead lives filled with misery and woe. From the very first page of this book when the children are at the beach and receive terrible news, continuing on through the entire story, disaster lurks at their heels. One might say they are magnets for misfortune.

In this short book alone, the three youngsters encounter a greedy and repulsive villain, itchy clothing, a disastrous fire, a plot to steal their fortune, and cold porridge for breakfast.

It is my sad duty to write down these unpleasant tales, but there is nothing stopping you from putting this book down at once and reading something happy, if you prefer that sort of thing.

With all due respect,
Lemony Snicket[8]

Can you imagine anybody reading that and *not* wanting to read the book? By making the story contained between those covers sound as horrible as possible—and funny as well (a disastrous fire *and* itchy clothing?)—Handler (or is it Snicket?) virtually guaranteed himself a large reading audience.

There is, undoubtedly, still one question remaining: Where did Lemony Snicket come from? Once again, his origins can be traced back to Handler's first novel, *The Basic Eight*. While writing that book, Handler had to do research, contacting right-wing organizations and such to get pamphlets from them and learn what made them tick. One day, he was on the phone speaking to one group's representative, who asked what name he should send the documents to. Not wanting to use his own name, Handler blurted out "Lemony Snicket!" The name stuck.

> It became a running joke with me and my friends; they gave me Lemony Snicket business cards one year, we invented a drink called the Lemony Snicket . . . . And when I started writing the children's books, and the character of the narrator emerged and my editor and I decided I needed a pseudonym, well, I'd had a pseudonym all along. And now I'm on the *New York Times* bestseller lists for a book by Lemony Snicket.[9]

THE BAD BEGINNING

The first book, *The Bad Beginning*, lays the groundwork for the series. After the narrator's warning of terrible events to come, and a description of the three Baudelaire children—Violet, the oldest, who liked to skip rocks and invent things; Klaus, the middle child who liked to read; and Sunny, the infant, who liked to bite things—the plot is quickly set into motion with the introduction of Mr. Poe, a banker and friend of Mr. and Mrs. Baudelaire, who meets them on the beach bearing sad news:

"Your parents," Mr. Poe said, "have perished in a terrible fire." The children didn't say anything. "They perished," Mr. Poe

Did you know...

Compared to the Harry Potter book series, there has been little merchandising of Lemony Snicket products. Why is that?

First of all, there is the kind of material associated with *A Series of Unfortunate Events*. What kind of meal would a fast-food place sell as an "un-Happy Meal?" Second of all, there is Handler's own mixed feelings about merchandising. While he remembers when he was a kid how much fun he had playing with the toys associated with the film *Star Wars*, there is also a part of him that would like the books to stand on their own as literature.

So, while there has been some merchandising, particularly in association with the film, such as a video game, a card game, and a board game, the items that Handler remains the most pleased with are probably the most simple: A Band-Aid that was given away in conjunction with *The Hostile Hospital* that simply said "Unfortunate Event" and a series of greeting cards that said things like "Why haven't you called?" and "It's all downhill from here!"

said, "in a fire that destroyed the entire house. I'm very, very sorry to tell you this, my dears."[10]

With that, the first in a series of what can only be called truly unfortunate events, the lives of the Baudelaire children would never be the same again. Mr. Poe becomes the executor of their parents' estate. "That means I will be handling their enormous fortune and figuring out where you children will go. When Violet comes of age, the fortune will be yours, but the bank will take charge of it until you are old enough."[11] But until Violet is old enough, the Baudelaire children, according to their parents' will, are to be raised by the relative who is the closest to them geographically. The man was Count Olaf, who is "either a third cousin four times removed or a fourth cousin three times removed."[12]

Count Olaf, an actor who travels the world with various theater companies, is the villain of the series. Olaf sets the orphans to work in his house, all the while busily plotting along with his theatrical troupe to deprive the orphans of their inheritance. Snicket (or is it Handler?) describes the troupe as follows:

> There was a bald man with a very long nose, dressed in a long black robe. There were two women who had bright white powder all over their faces, making them look like ghosts. Behind the woman was a man with very long and skinny arms, at the end of which were two hooks instead of hands. There was a person who was extremely fat and who looked like neither a man nor a woman.[13]

In the first book of the series, Count Olaf's plot is fiendishly clever. He forces Violet to perform with him in the play *The Marvelous Marriage* by Al Funcott. But instead of an actor, it will be a real judge who is tricked into performing what the Count hopes will be a legal marriage between him and Violet, which would place him, as her husband, in charge of her fortune!

Fortunately the orphans are able, by spunk, initiative, quick thinking (Violet who is right handed, signed the marriage license with her left hand, which is not, as the law required "in her own hand," thus nullifying the marriage), and Sunny's sharp teeth, to thwart Count Olaf's nefarious plot.

Reviewers took notice that a new voice was being heard in children's literature. A reviewer for *Publishers Weekly* noted, "The author uses formal, Latinate language and intrusive commentary to hilarious effect," adding that he "paints the satire with such broad strokes that most readers will view it from a safe distance."[14]

Some of you, no doubt, will be wondering exactly what the reviewer writing for *Publishers Weekly* meant. "Formal, Latinate language," means that Handler (or is it Snicket?) chose to write his book in a very stiff, somewhat dated style, which has the effect of making the events described seem even funnier. "Intrusive commentary," means that the narrator, Lemony Snicket, on more than one occasion breaks into the narrative line to speak directly to the reader, offering his opinions on what is happening in the story. There will be more on this topic later.

At any rate, *A Bad Beginning* was enough to earn Handler the respect of reviewers and audiences alike. It was just a beginning, and not a bad one at that. And as each new book was published, the audience continued to expand. Before he knew it, Daniel Handler would be the next big children's book superstar.

From left, Lemony Snicket (Daniel Handler) and illustrator Brett Helquist promote The End *in New York City in October 2006. Because of the popularity of* A Series of Unfortunate Events, *Helquist's illustrations have appeared not only in the books, but also on other products related to the series, including audiobook covers, calendars, and the like.*

6

Success

For various personal and legal reasons, I began researching the terrible things that happened to the three Baudelaire children following the deaths of their parents. The good people at HarperCollins offered to publish my findings, both as cautionary tales and for the general good.

–Lemony Snicket[1]

IN 1999, THE FIRST two books of *A Series of Unfortunate Events*, *The Bad Beginning* and *The Reptile Room*, were published. Three additional titles in the series were published in 2000: *The Wide Window*, *The Miserable Mill*, and *The Austere Academy*. And yet another three titles came out in 2001: *The*

Ersatz Elevator, *The Vile Village*, and *The Hostile Hospital*, and Lemony Snicket (or is it Daniel Handler?) had five books on the *New York Times*' children's best-seller list.

Just three years later, in September 2004, it was announced that over 25 million copies of the books had been sold worldwide and had been translated into 30 languages. Obviously, Handler was doing something right. His books had struck a chord among young readers, who were anxious to read as much about the adventures of the Baudelaire orphans as Handler (or was it Snicket?) was willing and able to write.

The first seven books of the series fall into a familiar yet comforting pattern. Count Olaf disguises himself, finds the children in whatever home Mr. Poe has placed them in, and, along with his accomplices, attempts to steal their fortune. In the later books in the series, the roles are reversed: the orphans are the ones who adopt various disguises while on the run from the police after they have been framed by Count Olaf. And, as always, the orphans attempt to get help from the hapless Mr. Poe, but Mr. Poe is always oblivious to their danger, and of course, the orphans are always, well, suffering through a series of highly unfortunate events.

For example, in the second book in the series, *The Reptile Room*, it appears, at least for a moment, that the brave trio will find happiness living with their uncle, Dr. Montgomery Montgomery, a kind-hearted herpetologist. Unfortunately for the orphans, their chance for happiness is destroyed by the arrival of Count Olaf. Writing for *Booklist*, Susan Dove Lempke worried that the "droll humor, reminiscent of Edward Gorey's" (astute readers will remember that the young Daniel Handler was a big fan of Gorey) "will be lost on some children; others may not enjoy the old-fashioned storytelling style that frequently addresses the reader directly and includes definition of terms."[2]

Of course, what Lempke failed to realize that it was precisely because of Handler's droll humor and old-fashioned storytelling style that *A Series of Unfortunate Events* was (and remains) so popular. In fact, many times adult reviewers fail to appreciate that young readers' tastes can be more advanced then they are generally given credit for! However, Lempke did go on to add that "plenty of children will laugh at the over-the-top satire; hiss at the creepy nefarious villains; and root for the intelligent, courageous, unfortunate Baudelaire orphans."[3]

In the next book, *The Wide Window*, the orphans have found refuge with their elderly Aunt Josephine who lives on Lake Lachrymose (here, lachrymose means "causing tears or crying"). Josephine is perhaps not the best person to be chosen as the protector of three young orphans being chased by the evil Count Olaf. She is afraid of anything and everything, as she makes clear in her first words to her new wards:

> "This is the radiator," Aunt Josephine said, pointing to a radiator with a pale and skinny finger. "Please don't ever touch it. You may find yourself very cold here in my home. I never turn on the radiator, because I am frightened it might explode, so it often gets chilly in the evenings."[4]

Not only is dear Aunt Josephine afraid of radiators, she is also afraid of, among other things, welcome mats, telephones, sofas, burglars, turning on the stove (which means chilled cucumber soup for dinner on a cold night), and realtors. Given, however, that this is a book by Lemony Snicket, Aunt Josephine does not survive the length of the book, as she is pushed into the leech-infested waters of Lake Lachrymose by Count Olaf in yet another attempt to get his hands on the orphans' fortune.

Things go, if possible, from bad to worse in the fourth book in the series, *The Miserable Mill*. As Lemony Snicket said himself in his traditional letter to the reader:

> I hope, for your sake, that you have not chosen to read this book because you are in the mood for a pleasant experience. If this is the case, I advise you to put this book down instantaneously, because of all the books describing the unhappy lives of the Baudelaire orphans, *The Miserable Mill* might be the unhappiest yet. Violet, Klaus, and Sunny Baudelaire are sent to Paltryville to work in a lumbermill, and they find disaster and misfortune behind every log. The pages of this book, I'm sorry to inform you, contain such unpleasantries as a giant pincher machine, a bad casserole, a man with a cloud of smoke where his head should be, a hypnotist, a terrible accident resulting in injury, and coupons.[5]

Despite the truly unfortunate events described in *The Miserable Mill*, reviewers enjoyed what they read. Writing in *Booklist*, Carolyn Phelan noted that "the story is deliciously mock-Victorian and self-mockingly melodramatic," and praised both the illustrations and "the author's many asides to the reader" both of which "underscore the droll humor. . . . Another plum for the orphans' fans."[6]

Adding to the chorus of praise, Sharon R. Pearce wrote in the *School Library Journal* that "this is for readers who appreciate this particular kind of humor."[7] (Readers—what do you think she means when she says "this particular kind of humor?") Pearce went on to add that Handler's kind of humor "exaggerates the sour and makes anyone's life seem sweet in comparison."[8] (Again readers—do you think like that when you are reading the books? Do you think: "Gosh, my life might be bad, but at least it is not as bad as the Baudelaire orphans' lives?")

Indeed, sometimes, it seems that adults, despite the positive reviews for *A Series of Unfortunate Events*, find it

Did you know...

Daniel Handler made a mistake in writing the first book of *A Series of Unfortunate Events* that influenced how the series ended. When planning out the series, Handler had originally thought to have the Baudelaire orphans return to Count Olaf's house in the twelfth book of the series, *The Penultimate Peril*, where they would find some information vital to solving the mysteries surrounding their lives.

However, way back in the first book of the series, *The Bad Beginning*, in a scene when the three children are locked in a room, Handler had written this simple sentence: "Klaus goes through all of Count Olaf's papers." So if, of course, they had already gone through "all of Count Olaf's papers," why would they have to go back to the Count's house and do it again? As Handler said, "It made kind of a mess of things . . . I had to change a huge part of the plan all because of this one sentence."*

*Amy Benter, "An Unfortunate Demise," Salon.com, October 28, 2006, http://www.salon.com/books/int/2006/10/18/handler.

difficult to believe that young readers enjoy the books as much as they do. And, indeed, the series has come under fire from some critics and school districts for its dark themes and comic use of violence. The criticism, however, was far less than Handler expected when he began working on the series: "We waited for the publishing house to hate it and then we at the publishing house waited for the librarians to hate it, and then we all waited for children to hate it."[9]

None of which happened, although his books were banned for a time in Decatur, Georgia, where Handler's planned visit was also canceled. What were the objections of the school's elementary teachers? Some objected to the hint of incest when Count Olaf tried to marry his niece Violet, and others objected to the use of the word "damn" in *The Reptile Room*. Handler responded that the word's use was "precipitated by a long discussion of how one should never say this word, since only a villain would do so vile a thing! This is exactly the lily-liveredness of children's books that I can't stand."[10]

But, despite the occasional objection, it is clear from the series' popularity that Handler has found a way to appeal both to young readers and adult readers alike. How does he do it? What is it about *A Series of Unfortunate Events* that makes it stand out and has helped it sell more than 55 million copies worldwide?

WHAT MAKES THE BOOKS A TREAT FOR YOUNG AND OLD ALIKE?

Obviously, first and foremost is the sheer pleasure of reading Handler's stories. He simply knows how to tell a good story, one that keeps the reader interested and anxious to know what is going to happen next. Without that skill, without that ability to tell a suspenseful narrative, nothing else really matters. But Handler has other skills besides just being a good storyteller. It is the way he tells a story, the way he weaves his themes and concepts throughout the books, the way he plays with language and the way he plays with the narrative and classic literature that makes reading him a joy for all.

One way that Handler gives pleasure to his readers is in the structure of the books. The majority of the books in the series begin immediately where the previous book ended. Not only that, but each of the first seven books follow the same pattern: each book is 13 chapters long (with the exception of *The End*, which has 14 chapters); and in each book the Baudelaires find themselves in a new yet horrible situation and faced with a new predicament and a new guardian.

The location of the crucial section of each book is given away in the title of the book. And, in each book, Handler gives each of the Baudelaire orphans a chance to use his or her own special talent: Violet gets to invent something, Klaus finds important information in a book, and Sunny gets to bite something, or, in the later books, uses her culinary skills. (There is one exception to this rule. In *The Miserable Mill*, Violet and Klaus swap roles: Klaus becomes the inventor, and Violet the researcher.)

By using a familiar and recognizable structure in his books, Handler gives the reader a sense of pleasure in the predictability of his narrative. But at the same time, Handler challenges his readers in each book with his use of language, in the way he comments on the narrative, and in his use of allusions.

Indeed, critics, teachers, librarians, and parents unite in their praise for Handler's use of language. As the narrator of the stories, Lemony Snicket often uses big, unfamiliar words in telling the Baudelaires' story. But unlike most writers, who would expect the reader to drag out a dictionary and look up the words they do not know, Snicket explains the words and analogies he uses, often in excruciatingly humorous detail.

When explaining a word that the reader may not know, he typically says something like "a word which here means. . ." Or, on occasion, when an adult person says what the word means, Klaus says that he and his siblings *know* what the word means, unless Klaus sees that there is no point in saying so. For example:

Mr. Poe:____(fill in the blank), by the way means_____ (add the definition)

Klaus: We know what _____ (fill in the blank) means.

Why did Handler take the approach of using his book to introduce new words to young readers?

I just like a lot of words, and I wanted to put them in these books. And as I was writing them—when I was writing the first book, it would occur to me that maybe aberrant was a word that wasn't known to many third-graders. And so then it seemed to fit right into this mock moralizing tone that the narrator would stop, often at very, very suspenseful moments, and define the word in a way that was hopelessly bound to that individual context. And so it makes me very happy to know that now, I mean, there are sort of millions of fourth-graders who know what the word "ersatz" means . . . that really excites me . . . I just love these words and I just wanted to put them in my books. There are not enough books that have the word "corpulent," in my opinion.[11]

Snicket's narration teaches new words to young readers and, as narrator, Snicket often interrupts some of the book's most exciting scenes to explain the very elements of writing. In *The Reptile Room*, for example, Uncle Montgomery Montgomery explains to the orphans that "I promise that if you take time to learn the facts, no harm will come to you here in the Reptile Room,"[12] Snicket then breaks into the narrative to explain:

> There is a type of situation, which occurs all too often and which is occurring at this point in the story of the Baudelaire orphans, called "dramatic irony." Simply put, dramatic irony is when a person makes a harmless remark, and someone else who hears it knows something that makes the remark have a different, and usually unpleasant, meaning. For instance, if you were in a restaurant and said out loud, "I can't wait to eat the veal marsala I ordered," and there were people around who knew that the veal marsala was poisoned and that you would die as soon as you took a bite, your situation would be one of dramatic irony. Dramatic irony is a cruel occurrence, one that is almost always upsetting, and I'm sorry to have it appear in this story, but Violet, Klaus, and Sunny have such unfortunate lives that it was only a matter of time before dramatic irony would rear its ugly head.[13]

Only Lemony Snicket (or is it Daniel Handler?) can make learning about literary terms such as "dramatic irony" both funny and educational!

Lemony Snicket breaks into the narrative in other ways as well. He interrupts the story to define clichés (overused phrases such as "blind as a bat"), often in excruciatingly funny detail, as he does in the fifth book of the series, *The Austere Academy*, to explain the phrase "prism of experience." He writes:

> Occasionally, events in one's life become clearer through the prism of experience, a phrase which simply means that things tend to become clearer as time goes on. For instance, when a person is just born, they usually have no idea what curtains are and spend a great deal of their first months wondering why on earth Mommy and Daddy have hung large pieces of cloth over each window in the nursery. But as the person grows older, the idea of curtains becomes clearer through the prism of experience. The person will learn the word "curtains" and notice that they are actually quite handy for keeping a room dark when it is time to sleep, and for decorating an otherwise boring window area. Eventually, they will entirely accept the idea of curtains, and may even purchase some curtains of their own, or venetian blinds, and it is all due to the prism of experience.[14]

He even breaks into the narrative at a particularly suspenseful point to say, for example, as he does in *The Reptile Room*:

> I *am* very, very sorry to leave you hanging like that, but as I was writing the tale of the Baudelaire orphans, I happened to look at the clock and realized I was running late for a formal dinner party given by a friend of mine, Madame diLustro. Madame diLustro is a good friend, an excellent detective, and a fine cook, but she flies into a rage if you arrive even five minutes later than her invitation states, so you understand that I had to dash off.[15]

Of course, the reader would never know that the narrator Lemony Snicket had to take a break from writing *unless* he

Numerous literary references have made their way into A Series of Unfortunate Events, *most notably the fact that the Baudelaire orphans are named after the famous nineteenth-century French poet Charles Baudelaire, seen here in a circa 1866 photo by Etienne Carjat.*

pointed it out in the story itself. And that, dear reader, is what makes it so funny. In an interview, Handler explained his reasons for the constant intrusions, "I was mostly just mocking the heavy-handedness that I remembered from kid's books that I didn't like as a child. That kind of mockery seems to really appeal to kids."[16]

Indeed, it is the voice of Lemony Snicket—cynical, mocking, despondent, and despairing of the orphans' future—that is perhaps the major element in the series' success. Handler, in creating Snicket's voice, somehow seems to break the general tone of darkness and despair with a wry sense of humor. For example, in his letter to the readers regarding the seventh book in the series, *The Vile Village*, Snicket uses humor to help lighten the mood and encourage the reader to look beyond the horrible events that the Baudelaire orphans will have to suffer through: "I can think of no single reason why anyone would want to open a book containing such unpleasant matters as migrating crows, an angry mob, a newspaper headline, the arrest of innocent people, the Deluxe Cell, and some very strange hats."[17]

The humor lies in the mix of unpleasant matters. An angry mob can definitely be considered an unpleasant matter. But can very strange hats?

As a narrator, Snicket also displays a dislike of the book's darker elements and seems to actually be squeamish and reluctant to describe some of the series' more unfortunate events. And while he seems to show nothing but admiration for the orphans' bravery and resilience in the face of constant danger and unhappiness, he often calls himself a coward and makes clear that he could not be as brave and resourceful as the Baudelaires. Is it possible that by emphasizing and praising the orphans' vitality and courage—especially in contrast to Lemony Snicket's lack of vitality and courage—that Handler is attempting to urge readers to find courage within themselves?

Indeed, throughout the books, the Baudelaire orphans are, despite their constant trials and tribulations, presented as worthy role models—resourceful, loyal, brave, free-thinking, and independent. In contrast, adults are shown to always obey authority and give in to mob psychology, peer pressure, ambition, and other ills. A special emphasis is also given to learning: those in the books who are "well read" are usually sympathetic characters, while those who shun books and education are villains.

One other factor that helps to explain the appeal of the series is the setting, which appears to be "timeless" with similarities to both the nineteenth century and the 1930s, although there are contemporary allusions to help confuse matters even more. The books' illustrations, masterfully done by Brett Helquist, give the books an Edward Gorey-like, nineteenth-century Victorian feel. So, in *The Hostile Hospital*, the orphans send a message via Morse code on a telegraph, while at the same time, in the Last Chance General Store, there is fiber-optic cable for sale. This blend of modern and old-fashioned items help to give the books their own particular appeal by creating their own fully realized yet fictional world.

And finally, one narrative quirk that appeals to both adults and young readers alike (although perhaps more to adults) is Handler's constant use of allusions. What allusions means in this case is the fact that many of the characters' names allude, or make an indirect reference to, other works of fiction, real people with connections to horror or works of horror, and even other literary works.

The life and work of the great nineteenth-century American author Edgar Allan Poe is often referenced in A Series of Unfortunate Events. *An early practitioner of the short story, Poe is highly regarded for his invention of the detective story and his tales of the macabre.*

Of these, the most obvious example is the Baudelaire orphans themselves, who are named after the French poet Charles Baudelaire. Sunny and Klaus also seem to take their first names from Claus and Sunny von Bulow. (Claus von Bulow was a British socialite accused of the attempted murder of his wealthy wife, Sunny.) Mr. Poe is undoubtedly a reference to the American author Edgar Allan Poe, known for virtually inventing the detective story as well as for his horror stories such as "The Tell-Tale Heart" and "The Cask of Amontillado."

(It is interesting to note that the real Charles Baudelaire actually met the real Edgar Allan Poe, and translated Poe's work from English to French. Edgar Allan Poe died from, among other things, tuberculosis, which is a disease of the lungs that involved coughing up blood—the fictional Mr. Poe is known, not surprisingly, for his terrible cough.)

Such allusions abound throughout the series. The Virginian Wolfsnake in *The Reptile Room* is an obvious reference to British author Virginia Woolf. Dr. Georgina Orwell in *The Miserable Mill* is an allusion to the author of *1984*, George Orwell. In *The Austere Academy*, the violin playing Vice Principal Nero refers to the Roman Emperor Nero, who is said to have played the fiddle while Rome burned; the auctioned-off Lot 49 is a reference to the novelist Thomas Pynchon's book *The Crying of Lot 49*, and the Akhmatova Bookstore is named after the great Russian poet Anna Akhmatova.

There are more. Auguste Dupin, the hero of Edgar Allen Poe's *The Purloined Letter* appears in *The Vile Village*. Heimlich Hospital in *The Hostile Hospital* is named after Henry Heimlich, the inventor of the anti-choking Heimlich maneuver. In the last book of series to date,

The End, the Baudelaires meet several people named after characters from *The Tempest*, William Shakespeare's play that takes place on an island under the control of the sorcerer, Prospero. *The Tempest* is widely believed to be the last play Shakespeare wrote alone.

Will young readers understand all the allusions that Handler utilizes in the series? Of course not. Are adult readers going to understand all the allusions that Handler utilizes in the series? Of course not. But by putting them in the books, Handler both amuses himself as a writer as well as keeps his readers, both young and old, on their toes.

Handler discussed his use of literary allusions in an interview with National Public Radio in 2001:

> Well, [the orphans] are cared for by Mr. Poe. At one point, they fall into the household of Jerome and Esme Squalor, who are named after J.D. Salinger's story of "For Esme with Love and Squalor." They attend Prufrock Preparatory School after the poem by T.S. Eliot. Yeah, they're pretty much surrounded by the world of books.
>
> I like the idea of a universe that was governed entirely by books. The Baudelaires find the solutions or what appear to be the solutions to their problems in libraries in each volume, and so there's sort of some heavy-handed or I hope mock heavy-handed propaganda, saying that all of life's difficulties can be solved within the pages of the right book.[18]

MORE TO DO

With their combination of dark humor, literary allusion and classic storytelling, *A Series of Unfortunate Events*, by the end of 2001, had made Daniel Handler a household name. Well, not exactly. The series had made Lemony Snicket a household name. Handler was still largely unknown. But as the decade progressed, it would be time for Daniel Handler to strike out in new career directions, as well to make changes in his personal life.

The Magnetic Fields, with Stephin Merritt on the right, performing at Cadogan Hall in London, England, in July 2008. When Merritt discovered he needed an accordion player to join his band to record 69 Love Songs, he turned to his friend Daniel Handler.

7

Film, Music, Politics, and the Baudelaire Orphans

WHEN ASKED WHY *A Series of Unfortunate Events* was so successful, Daniel Handler replied:

I have no idea. I am astonished. Pleasantly surprised would be a very, very mild understatement. I never thought such stories would be read by very many people and they have been. I used to have a half-baked philosophy as to why they reached such a large readership, but then I read this interview with [conservative television host] Bill O'Reilly where he gave more or less the same line of reasoning for his success. But obviously he's wrong. . . . And so I concluded that I must be wrong as well.[1]

But no matter the reason for the books' success, they *were* successful. So very successful in fact that Handler was in an enviable position for a writer, one in which money matters were no longer really a concern. He bought a house, a 1907 Victorian house on a high hill in San Francisco said to be on the windiest block in the entire city. He lives there still, with his wife and son, Otto, who was born sometime around Halloween 2003.

By the time of Otto's birth, the tenth book in the series, *The Slippery Slope*, was getting ready for publication, and within two years, in 2006, the last book in the series, *The End*, had been published. The series of unfortunate events had come to an end.

The curious thing was that while the "author" of *A Series of Unfortunate Events*, Lemony Snicket, was famous, Daniel Handler was not. Which was, in his view, not necessarily a bad thing, as he told *Redivider*: "The success of the Snicket series allows me to write full-time, in a house with a view of the sea. This is no bother at all. Besides, it's nice to hand over my credit card and attract no notice whatsoever."[2]

(What he means here, of course, is that his credit cards are, naturally, in the name of Daniel Handler, a name that is not, to say the least, a household name. After all, if you were not reading this book, would you know who Handler was?)

But with his success came new problems and dilemmas. Handler now had a lot of money; money that he felt guilty keeping when he saw so many around him in need. In June 2007, he wrote an essay for the *New York Times*, explaining his thoughts on the subject:

Let's start by saying I have a lot of money. I've acquired it by writing children's books about terrible things happening to orphans, and this seems like such a crazy and possibly monstrous way of acquiring money that I give a lot of it away. I mean, I guess it's a lot. Let me put it like this: My wife and I recently became obsessed with a Web site where you plug in the amount of money you made in a year and find out where you stand. If your salary equaled the amount of money my wife and I gave Planned Parenthood in one year, you'd be in the richest 1 percent in the world, which is pretty good. Still, there would be 60 million people richer than you, and that's a lot. They wouldn't fit in your home, for example, even though you'd have the sort of home that only the top 1 percent of people in the world can afford.[3]

So, giving away large amounts of money to organizations that he and his wife believed in did help assuage the guilt. And not only did his earnings as Lemony Snicket allow him the freedom to write full-time and to give freely to charitable organizations, it also allowed him to haul out his accordion and indulge his other artistic passion—music.

69 LOVE SONGS

Handler has been a fan of the musician Stephin Merritt for many years, and they had discussed the idea of working together on a musical. The timing was always off, however: Handler was just beginning to write *A Series of Unfortunate Events* and Merritt had just had the idea for his musical work, *69 Love Songs*. Merritt's musical idea was fairly straightforward: "I decided I'd write one hundred love songs as a way of introducing myself to the world. Then I realized how long that would be. So I settled on sixty-nine."[4]

Even still, writing 69 love songs is a lot of work. So, between *A Series of Unfortunate Events* and *69 Love Songs*, Handler's proposed collaboration was put on ice. But, when

Daniel Handler performs on the accordion at a book signing in New York in October 2006. On book tours he plays a wide variety of accordions, since one is always provided for him wherever he is contracted to make an appearance.

Merritt discovered he needed an accordion player to join his band Magnetic Fields for the recording of *69 Love Songs*, there was just one man he could turn to. Handler described the process in an interview with avclub.com:

> We said, "Well, as soon as we finish these little projects that we've both thought of individually, we'll work on this group thing," and then both those projects turned out to be much,

much bigger than we thought they would. So I ended up playing accordion simply because he was trying to get the album finished, and he knew I played the accordion, and if you play the accordion, you're usually the best accordion player anyone knows. So then being on the Magnetic Fields album led to a couple of other gigs. But I'm not very *good* at the accordion.

If I played guitar, I wouldn't be on anyone's album. But because I play the accordion and no one else does, I end up doing strange things.[5]

69 Love Songs was released in 1999 to rave reviews, and the working relationship between Handler and Merritt continued. Handler played accordion in the Merritt group The Gothic Archies, for which Merritt wrote, sang, and recorded

Did you know...

When Daniel Handler goes out on a book promotion tour, he often plays the accordion during his appearances in his role as Lemony Snicket's spokesman. But, since the time his accordion was damaged on an airplane and it was nearly impossible to find a replacement, it is now part of his agreement that there will be an accordion waiting for him wherever he is making an appearance! This gives him an opportunity to play on a wide variety of accordions, including one in Austin, Texas, which he was particularly fond of. Why? That accordion had brand new straps, and in other cities, the accordion he was playing had old leather straps, which, on one occasion, snapped right in half during a performance!

songs for the audiobook versions of Lemony Snicket's *A Series of Unfortunate Events*. (In 2006, a collection of all 13 songs, entitled *The Tragic Treasury*, was released.)

When doing readings, Handler often sings the songs to his young audience, especially a song about Count Olaf that was written to go with the first book in the series, *The Bad Beginning*. The song ends with the lyrics, "When you see Count Olaf, count to zero, then scream and run away. Scream, scream, scream and run away. Run, run, run, run, run, run, run, run or die. Die, die, die, die, die, die, die, die, die."[6] Handler went on to explain that at the readings:

> We usually encourage everyone's least favorite thing, audience participation, so during the part where I sing "run," everyone runs, and then the part where I sing "die," everybody slumps over on the floor. And really you haven't lived until you're standing in an independent bookstore watching a lot of eight- and nine-year-olds slump over as if dead.[7]

Handler has written songs for other groups as well, including the song "Radio," performed by One Ring Zero, as well as the lyrics to "The Gibbons Girl" by Chris Ewen's The Hidden Variable. And if writing books and music and playing the accordion weren't enough, Handler found time for yet another form of artistic expression: film.

MAKING THE MOVIE

In 2003, Handler wrote the screenplay for the film *Rick*, which was based on the opera *Rigoletto* by Giuseppe Verdi. Handler had written the screenplay years earlier, well before the publication of the first Lemony Snicket book. As he told the *A.V. Club*:

> Well, I wrote *Rick* before I was published, and I had no vision of it, really. It was just a story that occurred to me, and that

put its little claws into my brain, and I wrote it, and I showed it to a couple people, and they all said, "This is ghastly." One producer said that she liked it, and I said, "Well, knock yourself out. No one else wants to touch this thing."[8]

The film, which told of the tragic fall of a cursed Wall Street worker named Rick O'Lette (Rigoletto—get it?), starred Bill Pullman and Aaron Stanford. It did not fare well with either audiences or critics. The show business newspaper *Variety* called the film a "noxious little tale of Wall Street types whose amorality knows no limit, 'Rick' takes smarmy knowingness to ludicrous extremes . . . a shrill, one-note caricature . . . It all ends very badly, making for one of those films that makes one want to take a long shower afterward."[9]

There is one positive aspect about the film, however. If you look carefully, making an appearance as the "Pesky Waiter" is Daniel Handler himself!

The second film Handler was connected with got better reviews and reached a much wider audience. It was, of course, the film of his own best-selling books, curiously titled *Lemony Snicket's A Series of Unfortunate Events*. And the long and lengthy process of making the film was, in some ways, even more interesting than the movie itself.

Nickelodeon Movies purchased the film rights to Handler's books in May 2000, just one year after the first books had hit bookshelves. Director Barry Sonnenfeld (best known for his films *The Addams Family* and *Men in Black*) signed on in June 2002, and hired Handler to adapt the screenplay himself.

Handler set to work translating what he had put on the page to something that could be put on the big screen. He made eight attempts to write a screenplay that satisfied both himself and the film's producers. But when Barry

Although Daniel Handler had little to do with the film Lemony Snicket's A Series of Unfortunate Events, *he did contribute a commentary track to the DVD on which, as Lemony Snicket, he criticized the film extensively.*

Sonnenfeld left the project in January 2003 due to budgetary concerns and new director Brad Silberling took over, Handler's role would come to a rapid end. He recalled:

> I had written eight drafts of the screenplay when this changing-of-the-guard thing happened, and I said to the new producers, "I don't think I could write any more drafts." I guess I was sort of hoping they would say, "Well, that's okay, this last one is perfect." But instead, they said, "It's funny you should say that. We don't think you should write any more drafts either."[10]

So, Handler was no longer writing the film version of his own book: Robert Gordon was brought in to write what would become the final screenplay. The film, which starred Jim Carrey as Count Olaf (as well as various other roles), Liam Aiken as Klaus, Emily Browning as Violet, Kara and Shelby Hoffman as Sunny, Billy Connolly as Uncle Monty, Meryl Streep as Aunt Josephine, and Jude Law as the voice of Lemony Snicket, opened on December 17, 2004, to good reviews and rousing box office, ultimately earning over $200 million dollars worldwide.

But unlike the films based on the Harry Potter series, which were faithful to each individual book in the series, the film version of Handler's work was different. *Lemony Snicket's A Series of Unfortunate Events* was based on the first three novels in the series: *The Bad Beginning*, *The Reptile Room*, and *The Wide Window*. Fans of the books, as well as Handler himself, had mixed feelings about the film that, while not exactly true to Handler's books, was still a fairly entertaining romp, with a fully energetic performance from Jim Carrey. Handler said about the film:

> Well, for a while, it seemed like it was going to be the most exciting motion picture ever made . . . and then for a while it looked like it was going to be the *worst* movie ever made,

hopelessly embarrassing, and by the time it was finishing up, I was so grateful that it *wasn't* the worst movie ever made that I overlooked many things that might have otherwise upset me.[11]

Handler may not have been allowed to write the final screenplay, but in some ways, he did have the final word. When it came time to release the DVD of the film, Handler was asked to participate in the commentary track—an additional audio track that can be played along with the film, in which he and the film's director Brad Siberling discuss the film itself.

But instead of doing the commentary as Daniel Handler, he did it in character as Lemony Snicket, who went on to make a mockery of the proceedings, calling out Jude Law (who played Snicket in the film) as an imposter, as well as playing accordion and singing a song about leeches rather than attending to the movie at hand. Meanwhile, the film's director attempts to defend himself from Snicket's dismissal of the film.

In an interview with the *A.V. Club*, Handler described the process of making the track:

> We walked into a room, they showed us the movie, and we spoke into microphones. There was pretty much no prep whatsoever. And the director was immediately game, for which I am grateful, because if he had not been, I don't know *what* would have happened. Most people ask if we were intoxicated at the time, and we were not. . . .
>
> I'm not much of a fan of DVD commentaries myself, so this was my way of getting revenge.[12]

FINISHING THE SERIES

Within two years of the release of *Lemony Snicket's A Series of Unfortunate Events*, the books that inspired the film came to an end with the publication in 2005 of *The Penultimate Peril* and finally, in 2006, of the last book in the series, fittingly titled *The End*. After publishing 13 titles in less than a decade, was it difficult for Handler to end the series?

> Writing a book is always a tightrope walk, and always feels strange—one must care about something so thoroughly, in an embryonic stage, that one has made up to begin with. It was actually fairly easy to write the last volume of *A Series of Unfortunate Events*—it was the twelfth volume, in which the stage had to be cleared for *The End*, that proved difficult. *The Penultimate Peril* is more of an ending, with the recurrence of many characters from previous volumes, a few secrets revealed, and a finale of sorts. In *The End* I simply wanted to open up the story a bit, so that the lives of the characters would feel like lives, while the story would feel like a story, but the lives would move past the story, carrying their own questions. It's always difficult to talk about books this way without sounding like an idiot.[13]

With the publication of *The End* and the end of *A Series of Unfortunate Events*, it was now time for Daniel Handler to stand on his own, outside the formidable shadow of Lemony Snicket.

Colin Meloy, at left, and Daniel Handler talked about how they get their ideas for song and stories. Maloy of The Decemberists was interviewing Handler, who was on tour for his novel Adverbs.

What's Next?

THOSE WHO KNEW Daniel Handler only as the "creator" of Lemony Snicket, or perhaps as the author of *The Basic Eight* and *Watch Your Mouth*, would be shocked and pleasantly surprised by his next book, a novel for adults published in 2006 entitled *Adverbs*.

The book was five years in the making. Not that he was writing it full-time during that period. After all, there were Lemony Snicket books to be written, public appearances to make, and, as you know, accordions do not just play themselves. So it would be more than fair to say that it was written over the five years in a series of fits and starts. The first draft of the book totaled over 1,000 pages, and as he described it, "I couldn't find the rhyme or reason in what I was describing."[1]

It was only by putting it aside for a while and then coming back to it (a helpful hint that might prove useful to those of you who are aspiring writers) that he was able to look at it clearly and begin to cut away at it to find the structure hidden under the excessive verbiage. Was there anything of value lost amid all the editing? He responded that "the only useful thing about the cuts is that they were cut."[2]

Adverbs is set up as a collection of 17 narratives, all interconnected, and all from the points of view of different people in different sorts of love. Each of the titles is an adverb (the part of speech that modifies a verb, adjective, or other adverb) that gives the reader a clue as to what sort of love the people in the narrative are coping with. For example, some people are "wrongly" in love, others are "briefly" in love, and so forth. Instead of looking at who people are in love with, as do most such novels, *Adverbs* looks at the various ways that people *fall* in love.

Indeed, although *Adverbs* calls itself a novel, most people read it as a collection of short stories. But whatever genre it falls into, like *A Series of Unfortunate Events*, Handler happily breaks some of the most conventional rules of writing a novel. The narrative itself is filled with both half-truths and statements meant to mislead the reader; the point of view changes from story to story; characters reappear in the most unexpected places, and Handler (and most definitely *not* Lemony Snicket) makes appearances himself.

Any way you look at the book though, it is about love in all its splendid ways, and critics were nearly unanimous in their praise for the book. *Publishers Weekly* seemed to sum up what most critics were saying:

> The qualities that draw millions to Lemony Snicket—absurdity, wicked humor, a love of wordplay—get adulterated in this elegant exploration of love. Handler brings linguistic pyrotechnics to a set of encounters: gay, straight, platonic, and all degrees of dysfunctional. Amidst the deadpan ("Character description: Appropriately tall. Could dress better.") and the exhausting ("Love was in the air, so both of us walked through love on our way to the corner.") are moments of blithe poignancy. . . . Handler began his career with the coming-of-age novel *The Basic Eight*; this lovely, lilting book is a kind of After School Special for adults that dramatizes love's cross-purposes with panache: "Surely somebody will arrive, in a taxi perhaps, attractively, artfully, aggressively, or any other way it is done."[3]

It must have been a relief to Handler to know that after almost a decade of writing books for children that he could also write a book for adults that would get the critical attention and acclaim it deserved.

LYING LOW

After the publication of *The End* and *Adverbs*, Daniel Handler kept a fairly low profile. This is not to say that Handler did not find ways both to occupy himself and to satisfy his artistic urges. The year 2006 saw the world premiere of *The Composer Is Dead*, a work for orchestra with narration by Lemony Snicket. The piece was created with composer Nathaniel Stookey, who had gone to high school with Handler. The two had long lost touch, when, as Handler said:

I was actually being interviewed in an outdoor restaurant in San Francisco, and I was telling the interviewer that one of the things I liked about being in my home town of San Francisco was that I could run into people I knew from my childhood. And as soon as I said that—*suspiciously* soon—I ran into Nathaniel Stookey. We became reacquainted. . . . Through his

Did you know...

For the last several years (since 1999 actually), Daniel Handler has been hard at work on an adult novel about pirates.

It is said to be about modern people trying to become pirates in the old-school *Pirates of the Caribbean* way. Or, as Handler described it on Facebook, about a modern-day pirate who "wants to be an old-fashioned kind of pirate." But for those of you who think it will be a jolly rollicking kind of book, you obviously don't know Daniel Handler all that well. When asked in an interview how the book was coming along, he said it was still in the early stages, where he was optimistic that he could fix anything that was not perfect yet, and "as with the pirates themselves, despair and failure will set in soon enough."*

*"An Interview with Daniel Handler," October 2008, http://www.bookslut.com/features/2008_10_013548.php.

connections with the San Francisco Symphony, he got me a job narrating *Peter and the Wolf*. And *Peter and the Wolf* has very beautiful music, but an insipid, unpleasant story. So I suggested we could work on something that could introduce the orchestra to young people without introducing them to a really boring story about a grandfather and a wolf. And he agreed, and we did.[4]

Once again, Handler's dislike for traditional children's stories led him to create one of his own. What the two came up with was this:

It seems to me that the one thing everyone knows about composers, even if they don't know anything about classical music at all, is that all the composers are dead. And so I had the idea that the composer would be dead, and all the different sections of the orchestra would be questioned about his death, being that most symphony orchestras contain a few suspicious musicians. And it became the duty of the piece to ferret out who was the most treacherous member of the orchestra, who was responsible for the death of the composer.[5]

The work obviously struck a chord (so to speak) with listeners both young and old. Since its premiere, *The Composer Is Dead* has been recorded by the San Francisco Symphony, and performed by such illustrious orchestras as the Chicago Symphony, the Philadelphia Orchestra, and the Los Angeles Philharmonic.

In recent years, Handler busied himself in political activism, including sitting on the Board of Advisors of LitPAC, a political action committee which, through the organization of literary events, works to raise money to support Democratic politicians and to help register voters. Handler also, during this time, wrote a number of shorter books for young readers, including *Horseradish: Bitter Truths You Can't Avoid, The Lump of Coal*, and of course, that soon-to-be classic holiday story, *The Latke That Couldn't Stop Screaming*. Still, readers were not satisfied. They wanted more Lemony Snicket. And they wanted it as soon as possible.

Fortunately, their wishes are going to be fulfilled. On August 25, 2009, an announcement was made: A four-book-series, Lemony Snicket's first since *A Series of Unfortunate Events* was brought to an end in 2007, will begin being published in 2012. In making the announcement, Snicket's British publisher tried to put the best face possible on the sad news:

> As if the recession weren't bad enough, now British readers have the threat of a new series from Mr. Snicket hanging over them. As a responsible publisher, of course we shall put all our efforts into ensuring no child is exposed to yet more misery from Mr. Snicket's investigations.[6]

On November 11, 2009, Handler's American publisher, Little, Brown, announced that it would, indeed, be publishing the new four-part series, as well as Handler's first novel for young adults, scheduled to be published in 2012. As for Lemony Snicket himself, he had only this to say about his forthcoming books: "I can neither confirm nor deny that I have begun research into a new case, and I can neither confirm nor deny that the results are as dreadful and unnerving as *A Series of Unfortunate Events*."[7]

Since the publication of *The Bad Beginning* in 1999, Daniel Handler (or is it Lemony Snicket?) has become a force to be reckoned with in children's literature, writing books that in their dark humor, love of big words, and true dreadfulness, are like nothing else being written. It is comforting to know that there is still much to look forward to from the pen of Lemony Snicket (or it is Daniel Handler?).

CHRONOLOGY

1970 Daniel Handler is born in San Francisco, California, on February 28.

1988 Graduates from Lowell High School and decides to attend Wesleyan University.

1990 Wins the Academy of American Poets Prize.

1992 Graduates from Wesleyan University with a B.A. in 1992; receives Owin Fellowship.

1992–1999 While working on his first novels, supports himself with a series of jobs, including cocktail pianist, bartender, radio scriptwriter, movie reviewer, and freelance complainer.

1998 Marries long-time girlfriend Lisa Brown.

1999 Publication of Daniel Handler's first novel, *The Basic Eight*; Publication of Lemony Snicket's first two novels: *The Bad Beginning* and *The Reptile Room*; Release of *69 Love Songs*, composed by Stephin Merritt and performed by the Magnetic Fields, featuring the accordion playing of Daniel Handler.

2000 Publication of Daniel Handler's second novel, *Watch Your Mouth*; Publication of three Lemony Snicket novels: *The Wide Window*, *The Miserable Mill*, and *The Austere Academy*.

2001 Publication of three more Lemony Snicket novels: *The Ersatz Elevator*, *The Vile Village*, and *The Hostile Hospital*.

2002 Publication of Lemony Snicket's novel *The Carnivorous Carnival*.

2003 Birth of Daniel and Lisa's first child, Otto. Publication of Lemony Snicket's novel *The Slippery Slope*.

2004 Release of the film *Lemony Snicket's Series of Unfortunate Events*; publication of Lemony Snicket's novel *The Grim Grotto*.

2005 Publication of Lemony Snicket's novel *The Penultimate Peril*.

2006 Publication of the last of Lemony Snicket's *A Series of Unfortunate Events*, fittingly entitled *The End*; Publication of Daniel Handler's third novel, *Adverbs*; Debut of *The Composer Is Dead*, a piece for orchestra and narrator, with music by Nathaniel Stookey, and narration by Lemony Snicket.

2009 Announcement that Lemony Snicket will publish four additional novels, starting in 2012.

NOTES

Chapter 1

1 "Author Interview with Lemony Snicket," http://www.harpercollins.com/author/authorExtra.aspx?authorID=14581&displayType=interview.

2 Lemony Snicket, *Lemony Snicket: The Unauthorized Autobiography*, New York: HarperCollins, 2002, p. 3.

Chapter 2

1 "Lemony Snicket–Daniel Handler Biography," http://www.lemony-snicket-stuff.com/daniel_handler_biography.html.

2 "Meet the Writers: Lemony Snicket," http://www.barnesandnoble.com/writers/writerdetails.asp?cid=968086#interview.

3 "Lemony Snicket-Daniel Handler Biography," http://www.lemony-snicket-stuff.com/daniel_handler_biography.html.

4 Terry Gross, "Interview: Daniel Handler Talks about His Children's Books, 'A Series of Unfortunate Events,'" *Fresh Air*, NPR, December 10, 2001.

5 Sally Lodge, "Oh, Sweet Misery! Tales of Ultimately Unfortunate Kids Find an Eager Audience," *Publishers Weekly*, May 29, 2000, http://www.publishersweekly.com/article/CA168349.html.

6 Lemony Snicket, *The Bad Beginning*, New York: HarperCollins, 2000, p. 1.

7 Terry Gross, "Interview: Daniel Handler Talks about His Children's Books, 'A Series of Unfortunate Events,'" *Fresh Air*, NPR, December 10, 2001.

8 "Description of *The Blue Aspic*," http://www.amazon.com/Blue-Aspic-Edward-Gorey/dp/0764950622/ref=sr_1_1?ie=UTF8&s=books&qid=1262804196&sr=1-1.

9 Stephen Schiff, "Edward Gorey and the Tao of Nonsense," *New Yorker*, November 9, 1992; p. 89.

10 Kathleen Rooney, "Interview with Daniel Handler," *Redivider*, http://www.redividerjournal.org/interview-with-daniel-handler/.

11 Dino Buzzati, *The Bears' Famous Invasion of Sicily*, New York: The New York Review Children's Collection, 2004, back cover.

12 Ibid.

13 "Meet the Writers: Lemony Snicket," http://www.barnesandnoble.com/writers/writerdetails.asp?cid=968086#interview.

14 Terry Gross, "Interview: Daniel Handler Talks about His Children's Books, 'A Series of Unfortunate Events,'" *Fresh Air*, NPR, December 10, 2001.

15 Nadine Epstein, "The Jewish Secrets of Lemony Snicket,"

February 2007, http://
www.momentmag.com/
Exclusive/2007/2007-02/200702-
Handler.html.

16 Hayley Mitchell Haugen, *Daniel
Handler: The Real Lemony Snicket*,
Farmington Hills, MI: Kidhaven
Press, 2005, p. 18.

17 "Lemony Snicket-Daniel Handler
Biography," http://www.lemony-
snicket-stuff.com/daniel_handler_
biography.html.

18 Sally Lodge, "Oh, Sweet Misery!
Tales of Ultimately Unfortunate
Kids Find an Eager Audience,"
Publishers Weekly, May 29, 2000,
http://www.publishersweekly.com/
article/CA168349.html.

19 "An Interview with Daniel
Handler," *Something Jewish*,
http://www.somethingjewish.co.uk/
articles/1914_daniel_handler.
htm.

20 Daniel Handler, *The Basic Eight: A
Novel*, New York: Harper Perennial,
2006, pp. 37–38

Chapter 3

1 Kathleen Rooney, "Interview
with Daniel Handler," *Redivider*,
http://www.redividerjournal.org/
interview-with-daniel-handler/.

2 "An Interview with Daniel Handler,
a.k.a. Lemony Snicket, Part 1 and
Part 2," *About Creativity*, http://
about-creativity.com/2007/06/
an-interview-with-daniel-handler-
aka-lemony-snicket-part-1.php.

3 Ibid.

4 Ibid.

5 Ibid.

6 Ibid.

7 Kathleen Rooney, "Interview
with Daniel Handler," *Redivider*,
http://www.redividerjournal.org/
interview-with-daniel-handler/.

8 Ibid.

Chapter 4

1 Kathleen Rooney, "Interview
with Daniel Handler," *Redivider*,
http://www.redividerjournal.org/
interview-with-daniel-handler/.

2 "Meet the Writers: Lemony
Snicket," http://www.barnesand
noble.com/writers/writerdetails.
asp?cid=968086#interview.

3 Tasha Robinson, "An Interview
with Daniel Handler," *A.V. Club*,
November 16, 2005, http://www.
avclub.com/articles/daniel-handler,
13962/.

4 "Biography of Daniel Handler/
Lemony Snicket," *BookRags*, http://
www.bookrags.com/biography/
lemony-snicket-aya/.

5 "An Interview with Daniel
Handler," *Bookslut*, October
2008, http://www.bookslut.com/
features/2008_10_013548.php.

6 "Biography of Daniel Handler/
Lemony Snicket," *BookRags*, http://
www.bookrags.com/biography/
lemony-snicket-aya/.

7 Ibid.

8 Ibid.

9 Ibid.

10 Ibid.

11 Ibid.

12 "An Interview with Daniel
Handler," *Bookslut*, October
2008, http://www.bookslut.com/
features/2008_10_013548.php.

13 Ron Hogan, "An Interview with Daniel Handler," July 2000, http://www.beatrice.com/interviews/handler/.

14 "Biography of Daniel Handler/Lemony Snicket," *BookRags*, http://www.bookrags.com/biography/lemony-snicket-aya/.

Chapter 5

1 Lemony Snicket, *The Bad Beginning*, New York: HarperCollins, 2000, p. 1.

2 Tasha Robinson, "An Interview with Daniel Handler," *A.V. Club*, November 16, 2005, http://www.avclub.com/articles/daniel-handler,13962/.

3 Ginny Wiehardt, "Daniel Handler aka Lemony Snicket Discusses Unfortunate Events," About.com, http://fictionwriting.about.com/od/interviews/a/lemony_3.htm.

4 Tasha Robinson, "An Interview with Daniel Handler," *A.V. Club*, November 16, 2005, http://www.avclub.com/articles/daniel-handler,13962/.

5 "Biography of Daniel Handler/Lemony Snicket," *BookRags*, http://www.bookrags.com/biography/lemony-snicket-aya/.

6 Sally Lodge, "Oh, Sweet Misery! Tales of Ultimately Unfortunate Kids Find an Eager Audience," *Publishers Weekly*, May 29, 2000, http://www.publishersweekly.com/article/CA168349.html.

7 Tasha Robinson, "An Interview with Daniel Handler," *A.V. Club*, November 16, 2005, http://www.avclub.com/articles/daniel-handler,13962/.

8 Lemony Snicket, *The Bad Beginning*, New York: HarperCollins, 2000, back cover.

9 "Lemony Snicket–Daniel Handler Biography," http://www.lemony-snicket-stuff.com/daniel_handler_biography.html.

10 Lemony Snicket, *The Bad Beginning*, New York: HarperCollins, 2000, p. 8.

11 Ibid., p. 9.

12 Ibid., p. 15.

13 Ibid., pp. 47–48.

14 "Biography of Daniel Handler/Lemony Snicket," *BookRags*, http://www.bookrags.com/biography/lemony-snicket-aya/.

Chapter 6

1 "Author Interview with Lemony Snicket," http://www.harpercollins.com/author/authorExtra.aspx?authorID=14581&displayType=interview.

2 "Biography of Daniel Handler/Lemony Snicket," *BookRags*, http://www.bookrags.com/biography/lemony-snicket-aya/.

3 Ibid.

4 Lemony Snicket, *The Wide Window*, New York: Scholastic Inc., 2001, p. 15.

5 Lemony Snicket, *The Miserable Mill*, New York: HarperCollins, 2000, back cover.

6 "Biography of Daniel Handler/Lemony Snicket," *BookRags*, http://www.bookrags.com/biography/lemony-snicket-aya/.

7 Ibid.

8 Ibid.

9 Anna Vaux, "Move Over Harry Potter," *The Guardian*, December 4, 2001, http://www.guardian.co.uk/theguardian/2001/dec/04/g2/features11.

10 Ibid.

11 Terry Gross, "Interview: Daniel Handler Talks about His Children's Books, 'A Series of Unfortunate Events,'" *Fresh Air*, NPR, December 10, 2001.

12 Lemony Snicket, *The Reptile Room*, New York: HarperCollins, 2000, p. 31.

13 Ibid., pp. 31–32.

14 Lemony Snicket, *The Austere Academy*, New York: HarperCollins, HarperCollins, 2000, pp. 133–134.

15 Lemony Snicket, *The Reptile Room*, New York: HarperCollins, 2000, p. 27.

16 "Biography of Daniel Handler/Lemony Snicket," *BookRags*, http://www.bookrags.com/biography/lemony-snicket-aya/.

17 Lemony Snicket, *The Vile Village*, New York: HarperCollins, 2001, back cover.

18 Terry Gross, "Interview: Daniel Handler Talks about His Children's Books, 'A Series of Unfortunate Events,'" *Fresh Air*, NPR, December 10, 2001.

Chapter 7

1 Nadine Epstein, "The Jewish Secrets of Lemony Snicket," February 2007, http://www.momentmag.com/Exclusive/2007/2007-02-200702-Handler.html.

2 Kathleen Rooney, "Interview with Daniel Handler," *Redivider*, http://www.redividerjournal.org/interview-with-daniel-handler/.

3 Daniel Handler, "Adjusted Income," *New York Times*, June 10, 2007, http://www.nytimes.com/2007/06/10/magazine/10lives-t.html.

4 Interview, *San Francisco Bay Guardian*, September 1, 1999.

5 Tasha Robinson, "An Interview with Daniel Handler," *A.V. Club*, November 16, 2005, http://www.avclub.com/articles/daniel-handler,13962/.

6 Terry Gross, "Interview: Daniel Handler Talks about His Children's Books, 'A Series of Unfortunate Events,'" *Fresh Air*, NPR, December 10, 2001.

7 Ibid.

8 Tasha Robinson, "An Interview with Daniel Handler," *A.V. Club*, November 16, 2005, http://www.avclub.com/articles/daniel-handler,13962/.

9 Todd McCarthy, "Rick," *Variety*, October 14, 2003, http://www.variety.com/review/VE1117922127.html?categoryid=31&cs=1.

10 Tasha Robinson, "An Interview with Daniel Handler," *A.V. Club*, November 16, 2005, http://www.avclub.com/articles/daniel-handler,13962/.

11 Ibid.

12 Ibid.

13 "An Interview with Daniel Handler," *Bookslut*, October 2008, http://www.bookslut.com/features/2008_10_013548.php.

Chapter 8

1 "An Interview with Daniel Handler," *Something Jewish*, http://www.somethingjewish.co.uk/articles/1914_daniel_handler.htm.

2 "An Interview with Daniel Handler," *Bookslut*, October 2008, http://www.bookslut.com/features/2008_10_013548.php.

3 "Review of *Adverbs*," *Publishers Weekly*, http://www.amazon.com/Adverbs-Novel-P-S-Daniel-Handler/dp/0060724420/ref=sr_1_1?ie=UTF8&s=books&qid=1262804293&sr=1-1.

4 Zack Smith, "Daniel Handler, aka Lemony Snicket, Discusses His Music, Movies and Books," *Indy Week*, March 4, 2009, http://www.indyweek.com/gyrobase/Content?oid=oid%3A307143.

5 Ibid.

6 Alison Flood, "Lemony Snicket Threatens a 'Dreadful' New Series," *The Guardian*, August 25, 2009, http://www.guardian.co.uk/books/2009/aug/25/lemony-snicket-series.

7 Ibid.

WORKS BY LEMONY SNICKET (DANIEL HANDLER)

AS LEMONY SNICKET

1999 *The Bad Beginning; The Reptile Room; The Wide Window*

2000 *The Miserable Mill; The Austere Academy*

2001 *The Ersatz Elevator; The Vile Village; The Hostile Hospital*

2002 *The Carnivorous Carnival; Lemony Snicket: The Unauthorized Autobiography; The Baby in the Manger*

2003 *The Slippery Slope*

2004 *The Grim Grotto; The Lump of Coal*

2005 *The Penultimate Peril;* (as contributor) *Noisy Outlaws, Unfriendly Blobs, and Some Other Things That Aren't as Scary, Maybe, Depending on How You Feel About Lost Lands, Stray Cellphones, Creatures from the Sky, Parents Who Disappear in Peru, a Man Named Lars Farf, and One Other Story We Couldn't Quite Finish, So Maybe You Could Help Us Out*

2006 *The End; The Beatrice Letters; The Puzzling Puzzles; 13 Shocking Secrets You'll Wish You Never Knew About Lemony Snicket*

2007 *Horseradish: Bitter Truths You Can't Avoid; The Latke Who Couldn't Stop Screaming*

AS DANIEL HANDLER

1998 *The Basic Eight*

2000 *Watch Your Mouth*

2005 *How to Dress for Every Occasion, by the Pope*

2006 *Adverbs*

POPULAR BOOKS

ADVERBS

Daniel Handler's return to the adult market, *Adverbs* explores the world of love and relationships in all their messy, confused splendor, in a series of interconnected stories that stretch the definition of what a "novel" is.

THE BASIC EIGHT

In this, Daniel Handler's first book, he looks at events at Roewer High School, where the lives of "The Basic Eight," an exclusive clique, are turned upside down by alcohol, self-discovery, and murder

A SERIES OF UNFORTUNATE EVENTS

These are the books that made Lemony Snicket a household name. There are 13 books in all (at least to date), and they tell the tale of the Baudelaire orphans, the evil Count Olaf, the orphans' inheritance, and the mysterious V.F.D. With millions and millions of copies sold worldwide, it is Handler's (or is it Snicket's?) most popular and best known work.

POPULAR CHARACTERS

KLAUS BAUDELAIRE

The middle child of the Baudelaire orphans, Klaus, who loves to read, uses the knowledge he gains from books to help him and his sisters escape from Count Olaf's dastardly plots.

SUNNY BAUDELAIRE

The youngest of the Baudelaire orphans, Sunny uses her four sharp teeth, and later her culinary skills, to help defeat Count Olaf's fiendish schemes to get his hands on the orphans' inheritance.

VIOLET BAUDELAIRE

The oldest of the Baudelaire orphans, Violet loves to invent things and uses her skills as an inventor to protect herself, as well as her younger brother and sister, from the evil machinations of Count Olaf.

COUNT OLAF

An actor and distant relation of the Baudelaire children, easily recognized by his unibrow and his tattoo of the V.F.D. eye on his ankle (unless they're covered up as part of his series of disguises), Count Olaf has an unexplained and unhealthy fixation on the Baudelaire orphans. He spends his days tracking down the orphans wherever they go and is willing to do whatever fiendish acts are necessary to get his hands on their inheritance.

BIBLIOGRAPHY

Books and Articles

Benfer, Amy. "An Unfortunate Demise," Salon.com. October 28, 2006. Available online. URL: http://www.salon.com/books/int/2006/10/28/handler/index.html.

Buzzati, Dino. *The Bears' Famous Invasion of Sicily*. New York: New York Review Children's Collection, 2004.

Dr. Davis. "Defining Gothic," July 11, 2009. Available online. URL: http://www.teachingcollegeenglish.com/2009/07/11/defining-gothic.

De Lisle, Tim. "Not So Unfortunate: Tim De Lisle Meets Daniel Handler/Lemony Snicket," *The Guardian*. June 7, 2006. Available online. URL: http://www.guardian.co.uk/books/2006/jun/07/fiction.features11.

Elliot, Stephen. "Announcing LitPAC," April 3, 2006. Available online. URL: http://www.huffingtonpost.com/stephen-elliott/announcing-litpac_b_18399.html.

Epstein, Nadine. "The Jewish secrets of Lemony Snicket," February 2007. Available online. URL: http://www.momentmag.com/Exclusive/2007/2007-02/200702-Handler.html.

Flood, Alison. "Lemony Snicket Threatens a 'Dreadful' New Series," August 25, 2009. *The Guardian*, Available online. URL: http://www.guardian.co.uk/books/2009/aug/25/lemony-snicket-series.

Gross, Terry. "Interview: Daniel Handler Talks about His Children's Books, 'A Series of Unfortunate Events,'" *Fresh Air*, NPR, December 10, 2001.

Handler, Daniel. *The Basic Eight*. New York: Harper Perennial, 2006.

———. "Adjusted Income," *New York Times*, June 10, 2007. Available online. URL: http://www.nytimes.com/2007/06/10/magazine/10lives-t.html.

Haugen, Hayley Mitchell. *Daniel Handler: The Real Lemony Snicket*. Farmington Hills, Mich.: Kidhaven Press, 2005.

Hogan, Ron. "An Interview with Daniel Handler," July 2000. Available online. URL: http://www.beatrice.com/interviews/handler/.

Lodge, Sally. "Oh, Sweet Misery! Tales of Ultimately Unfortunate Kids Find an Eager Audience," *Publishers Weekly*, May 29, 2000. Available online. URL: http://www.publishersweekly.com/article/CA168349.html.

McCarthy, Todd. "Rick," *Variety*, October 14, 2003. Available online. URL: http://www.variety.com/review/VE1117922127.html?categoryid=31&cs=1.

Robinson, Tasha. "An Interview with Daniel Handler," *A.V. Club*, November 16, 2005. Available online. URL: http://www.avclub.com/articles/daniel-handler,13962/.

Rooney, Kathleen. "Interview with Daniel Handler," *Redivider*. Available online. URL: http://www.redividerjournal.org/interview-with-daniel-handler/.

Schiff, Stephen. "Edward Gorey and the Tao of Nonsense," *New Yorker*, November 9, 1992, p. 89.

Shulman, Dave. "Zam Zam With Lemony Snicket," *L.A. Weekly*. Available online. URL: http://www.laweekly.com/2004-12-16/news/zam-zam-with-lemony-snicket.

Smith, Zack. "Daniel Handler, aka Lemony Snicket, Discusses His Music, Movies and Books," *Indy Week*, March 4, 2009. Available online. URL: http://www.indyweek.com/gyrobase/Content?oid=oid%3A307143.

Snicket, Lemony. *The Austere Academy*. New York: HarperCollins, 2000.

———.*The Bad Beginning*. New York: HarperCollins, 1999.

———. *Lemony Snicket: The Unauthorized Autobiography*. HarperCollins, 2002.

———. *The Miserable Mill*. New York: HarperCollins, 2000.

———. *The Reptile Room*. New York: HarperCollins, 1999.

———. *The Vile Village*. New York: HarperCollins, 2000.

———. *The Wide Window*. New York: HarperCollins, 2007.

Vaux, Anna. "Move Over Harry Potter," *The Guardian*, December 4, 2001. Available online. URL: http://www.guardian.co.uk/theguardian/2001/dec/04/g2/features11.

Whiting, Sam. "Fortunate Events: Winds, Vertiginous Views and Snakes Converge in Lemony Snicket's Neck of the Woods," *SF Gate*, May 18, 2003. Available online. URL: http://www.sfgate.com/cgi-bin/article.cgi?f=/c/a/2003/05/18/CM116426.DTL.

Wiehardt, Ginny. "Daniel Handler aka Lemony Snicket discusses Unfortunate Events," About.com. Available online. URL: http://fictionwriting.about.com/od/interviews/a/lemony_3.htm.

Web Sites

"A Conversation with Daniel Handler." HarperCollins.com. Available online. URL: http://www.harpercollins.com.au/author/authorExtra.aspx?authorID=50018437&displayType=interview.

"An Interview with Daniel Handler, a.k.a. Lemony Snicket, Part 1 and Part 2," About Creativity. Available online. URL: http://about-creativity.com/2007/06/an-interview-with-daniel-handler-aka-lemony-snicket-part-1.php.

"An Interview with Daniel Handler," Something Jewish. Available online. URL: http://www.somethingjewish.co.uk/articles/1914_daniel_handler.htm.

"An Interview with Daniel Handler," Bookslut.com, October 2008. Available online. URL: http://www.bookslut.com/features/2008_10_013548.php.

"Author Interview with Lemony Snicket." HarperCollins.com. Available online. URL: http://www.harpercollins.com/author/authorExtra.aspx?authorID=14581&displayType=interview.

"Biography of Daniel Handler/Lemony Snicket," BookRags.com. Available online. URL: http://www.bookrags.com/biography/lemony-snicket-aya/.

"Biography of Lemony Snicket (Daniel Handler)," *Encyclopedia of World Biography*. Available online. URL: http://www.notablebiographies.com/news/Sh-Z/Snicket-Lemony-Daniel-Handler.html.

"Daniel Handler Author Biography." Lemony Snicket Stuff. Available online. URL: http://www.lemony-snicket-stuff.com/daniel_handler_biography.html.

"Description of *The Blue Aspic*." Amazon.com. Available online. URL: http://www.amazon.com/Blue-Aspic-Edward-Gorey/dp/0764950622/ref=sr_1_1?ie=UTF8&s=books&qid=1262804196&sr=1-1.

"Meet the Writers: Lemony Snicket." BarnesandNoble.com. Available online. URL: http://www.barnesandnoble.com/writers/writerdetails.asp?cid=968086#interview.

"Review of *Adverbs*," *Publishers Weekly*. Available online. URL: http://www.amazon.com/Adverbs-Novel-P-S-Daniel-Handler/dp/0060724420/ref=sr_1_1?ie=UTF8&s=books&qid=1262804293&sr=1-1.

FURTHER READING

Blair, David (editor). *Gothic Short Stories.* Hertfordshire, England: Wordsworth Editions, 2002.

Dahl, Roald. *The Best of Roald Dahl.* New York: Vintage, 1990.

Gorey, Edward. *Amphigorey.* New York: Putnam, 1972.

Snodgrass, Mary Ellen. *Encyclopedia of Gothic Literature.* New York: Facts on File, 2004.

Snyder, Zilpha Keatley. *The Changeling.* Backinprint.com, 2004.

PICTURE CREDITS

INDEX

Characters are listed by name followed by the title in parenthesis of the work in which they appear. Page numbers in *italics* indicate photos or illustrations.

ABOUT THE CONTRIBUTOR

DENNIS ABRAMS is the author of numerous books, including biographies of Barbara Park, Anthony Horowitz, Rachael Ray, Sandra Day O'Connor, and Che Guevara, all for Chelsea House. He attended Antioch College, where he majored in English and communications. He lives in Houston, Texas, with his partner of 21 years and his dog, Junie B.